The Cove

The Cove.

Mantawassuk

Bud Simpson

Bud Simpson

To order additional copies of this book, contact:
Xlibris Corporation
1-888-795-4274
www.Xlibris.com
Orders@Xlibris.com
85908

Contents

Dedication

A writer should always dedicate his first book to his wife and his mother; especially so for this book. My mother carried heavy burdens of poverty and abuse throughout her too short life. I dedicate it too, to my long suffering brother and sisters. My brother Trevor shared my joys of discovery in some of these essays, but sometimes one of my sisters; Joan, Dolores, or Linda, were there, also. Inspiration to write this book came from Bill Geagan, outdoors writer, author, and artist of a past era, and Tom Hennessey, outdoors writer, author, and artist of this era.

FOREWORD

"FOLLOWING BUD SIMPSON'S trail of words will take you back to a time when boys growing up in Maine's river towns didn't have much but didn't need much to master the art of 'making do.' With woods and waters at their doors, literally, they were educated and entertained in the grand theater of the great outdoors. Herein, then, are accounts of how a boy raised on the banks of Maine's most storied river, the Penobscot, grew, matured and prospered by learning, firsthand, lessons of patience, discipline, responsibility and respect for nature and its often harsh and unforgiving forces."

Tom Hennessey

Outdoors columnist for the *Bangor Daily News*.

Tom Hennessey, now retired, still writes an occasional column for the *Bangor Daily News*. Not only is he an artist with words; painting a mental landscape so vivid you can visualize it in your mind and feel it in your soul, he is also an accomplished artist with pencil, pen and ink, and watercolor. His drawings and paintings of his favorite subject, "The Grand Theater of the Great Outdoors," are well known throughout the nation. He is also the author of two eloquently written books about his favorite subject. His first book, *Feathers and Fins*, was published in 1989 by the Amwell

Press. His second book, *Handy to Home: a Lifetime in the Maine Outdoors*, was published by the Silver Quill Press in Camden, Maine in 2000. Both books, illustrated with his own artistic works, showcase his superb abilities as both a writer and an artist.

I strove with none, for none was worth my strife.
Nature I loved and, next to nature, Art.
I warmed both hands before the fire of life,
It sinks, and I am ready to depart.

Walter Savage Landor

INTRODUCTION

I DON'T KNOW what it is that would make a person feel his life or a period in it was so unique that it is worth the effort to put it down on paper. Perhaps I feel this urge so strongly because the geographic area I want to write of no longer exists as it was in the days when it was such an important part of my life. Also, like this area, I am not the same person today that I was when these events took place.

Perhaps, also, this could be just an attempt to grasp at a small bit of immortality . . . something that will remain after I am gone. No feeling person wants to leave this small planet behind with the nagging thought in his mind that all was for naught; I contributed nothing.

With a little bit of luck, someone may even receive a small bit of pleasure from reading my words and, possibly, may even learn something. If nothing else, these words will preserve some of the history of the area in which I grew up.

I recognize the fact that no two people see the same event in the same way. This is especially so when the events must be dredged up from fifty or more years of storage deep within your mind. Perhaps others will view these stories in a different light or in a different way, but it matters not, for undaunted, I shall forge ahead. I'll record them as faithfully as I can and hope they will retain their basic veracity and the real truth has only mellowed over the years as with a good wine.

It will be obvious I came from a poor family, but if I had not, events in my life would not have been the same and some of these events would not have occurred at all. It would serve no useful purpose to dwell on the reasons for our poverty, so please accept the fact that our poverty was acute and prolonged and had a profound effect on *all* the members of my family. Because the physical appearance of the area in which my story takes place has changed so drastically over the years, it will be simpler to write the story as though the area still exists as it was then. In the final pages, I'll bring you up to date as to what the area is like today. So come with me, walk in my footsteps and I'll tell you about Mantawassuk, the Cove.

*   *   *

I wrote the above introduction in 1982 while living on the Levensellar Road in the Town of East Holden, Maine. This home was just a Paul Bunyan stone's throw from the house where I was born on North Main Street in Brewer, Maine on December 27th in 1934. Since 1982, many things have happened in my life and I find myself picking up the pieces one more time here in the small city of Logan in the southeastern portion of the State of Ohio in the year 2005. As I read over the notes and pages of my unfinished manuscript, I once again feel the urge to write of my early life in the State of Maine. So, I happily pick up the pieces one more time and I am determined to complete the job this time. But, as a wiser person than I once said, "If you want to hear God laugh, tell him your plans for the next two years." Well, I won't be telling Him my plans, but if He finds out, maybe He will feel sorry for me and will not let life interfere with my little project this time until it is finished.

CHAPTER ONE

The Earliest Days

THE SIMPSON FAMILY was the poorest family on North Main Street; possibly in the whole City of Brewer; and at times it seemed to us, in the whole damned State of Maine!

We lived in an abbreviated version of a two-story frame house; mostly frame . . . not much house. This house was never finished beyond the tarred paper stage except for an aborted attempt at putting on some imitation brick siding at one point. The second story and the back part of the house were additions to a finished bungalow that my father had built when he and my mother were first married. This bungalow was built, I am told, from lumber cut from logs and boards that my father salvaged from the Penobscot River during the spring freshets. The river flows directly behind the property a few hundred feet from the house.

He would go out on the river in a rowboat and spear the logs with a logging tool called a pick pole. This is a long, sharp, metal tipped pole about ten or twelve feet long. With this he speared the logs and hauled them ashore behind the boat. This type of ambition was apparently killed in my father in later years when alcohol became the dominant urge in his life and was probably the principle reason that the house was never finished beyond the stage described.

The only barrier between the severity of the Maine winters and the interior of the house was a one-inch layer of wood and a tattered layer of tarred paper. At night after the fires in the wood stoves had expired and the last embers had died, the cold of the winter nights, like icy little demons, would steal through the many cracks and crevices in the exterior of our house. In no time at all, it got to be nearly as cold inside as it was outside.

In the morning, the water bucket beside the sink in the kitchen might have an inch or two of ice in it and the glass of water beside my bed might be frozen solid. The window panes would be covered with icy crystals of frost from the moisture that is created from the burning of green, wet wood that we had burned in the big, black kitchen stove. I would stick my head out from under the blankets and old coats piled on top of my bed and could make a judgment as to how cold it might be by just how high my frozen breath could be blown in my arctic-like room.

After the kitchen stove had been lit, we all huddled next to it, trying to absorb as much heat as we could before it gave up its energy to the frigid air in the rest of the house. If you moved only a few feet from the stove on mornings like this, it seemed as if the heat could never reach you, so we stayed as close to the stove as possible. We rotated our bodies as if we were on a spit; warming front and back as best we could. Eventually the kitchen would warm up enough for us to gather our courage and attempt to eat breakfast, such as it was.

Breakfast was always very simple, usually toast and cocoa, when available. The bread or biscuits were toasted on the cast iron covers of the old kitchen stove. Care had to be taken or you might end up with a piece of burnt bread instead of toast. You never put the bread on the front covers over the fire. The secret was to put it on one of the back covers over the oven. I was very clever at selecting which one that might be. Always the gentleman, I would let my brother or sisters toast their bread first, then I could then see which of the covers was delivering the best toast that morning. I have never liked the dry, charcoal taste of burnt toast.

I have no recollection of ever going into a store to try on new clothes as a child. New clothes were a rarity in those early years. We were not the only kids in the neighborhood to wear hand-me-downs, but it seemed that we were the only kids who wore *only* hand-me-downs. So, the coat is a little large? Don't worry; it will fit you better next year. The boots are too big? We'll stuff some paper into the toes. They'll fit you then.

I didn't really mind the hand-me-downs too much, but sometimes we got the hand-me-downs that had been handed down to other kids in the neighborhood. It doesn't do a young ego much good to wear the jacket Jimmy wore last year and Johnny had worn the year before. It seemed as if a good jacket received immortality of sorts in our neighborhood and was reincarnated on the backs of many.

We had no indoor plumbing or running water in our house until I was in my late teens. The house was wired for electricity, but there were times when the kerosene lamps and lanterns were put to good use. Electric utility companies never have been too forgiving or understanding when their bills were not paid.

All our drinking water was carried by hand in galvanized, steel buckets from a rock lined spring with a wooden cover over it to keep out falling leaves and the occasional falling animal. The spring was located on our next door neighbor's property more than a hundred yards from our house. Rainwater was collected in a large, wooden barrel located under the eaves of the house. My mother used this water to wash the laundry during the warmer months of the year.

Laundry was enough of a chore under these conditions at any time, but in the winter it became a job of tremendous proportions. During these winter months, we had to collect snow in buckets and bring it into the house to be melted in a large galvanized tub set on the kitchen stove. As the snow melted, more was added until the tub was finally filled with water. After this water was heated, it was then transferred pot by pot to one of my mother's two somewhat modern conveniences, an old agitator type washing machine with a reversible wringer. While the clothes were washing in the machine, back on the stove went the laundry tub and more snow was melted. This time it was to be used for rinsing the clothes.

The tub would have to be lifted off the stove when its content of water was hot enough, so it was not filled with water at this time, but only with an amount that we could handle without too much difficulty. All the surplus pots and pans that would fit on top of the stove were then pressed into service for melting the additional snow that would be required to fill the tub for rinsing.

When the clothes had washed long enough, they were passed through the wringer and caught in the tub of rinse water. My mother would the slosh the clothes around in the tub by hand until she felt they were rinsed enough. The wringer was then swung away from the washer and over the rinse tub. The clothes passed through the wringer once more and dropped into a wicker laundry basket. If there were more clothes to wash, this rinse water was used one more time to do another load of clothes and the cycle was repeated again.

Then, of course, the clothes had to be hung out to dry, regardless of the temperature, on the clothesline out behind the house. At times this was the worse part of this project. My mother's hands would get so cold and chapped that she could, at times, hardly pin the clothes in place.

The clothes would eventually dry to one degree or another, even in the coldest of weather, probably by the same principle that is used to freeze dry foods today. Then the clothes would be brought into the house and my mother's second modern convenience would be brought into play, her electric iron.

Ironing served two purposes; to make the clothes presentable and to help dry out as much of the remaining moisture as possible. This all took place back in the 1940's before the days of wash and wear, so nearly every thing had to be ironed or pressed. For those of you who are too young to know, pressing was done by laying a piece of cloth over the garment. Then you sprinkled the cloth with water and ironed the garment through the damp cloth.

When I think back over everything, all the things my mother was required to do seem all the more amazing because my mother was a tiny woman; an inch under five feet tall and never weighing more than ninety pounds in her entire life. She was, however, a giant in the mother department. I hear the women of today complaining because life is so stressful with a couple of children to take care of. They should walk a mile in my mother's shoes. They probably would stop walking after a hundred yards or so.

It is difficult enough to raise five children under the very best of conditions, but under the conditions she had to endure, it had to have been an extremely trying experience. My mother was not a complainer though, and she did it all simply because it had to be done and she was the only one around to do it.

If you lived as we did, diversions became an important part of your life. Diversions allowed you to escape for the moment from the difficult conditions of daily life. Fortunately for me, I had many ways to escape. I could sit and draw pictures for hours. Drawing allowed me to mentally have that fishing rod that we could not afford. My dreams could come alive on paper. I would make models of anything that struck my fancy . . . airplanes, boats, houses, rifles or pistols. All from scratch, of course; there was no money to buy kits.

My main diversion, and my brother Trevor's as well, was fishing. From the time we were old enough to leave the house on our own, most of our time was spent at Johnson Brook or The Cove it formed where it enters the Penobscot River, or on the river itself. It is impossible for me to think of my formative years without thinking of these three areas; but of The Cove in particular.

One of the reasons fishing was important to me was because it produced a very important by-product . . . food! Personally, food was of secondary importance to me. The act of fishing and the pleasure it brought to me was the primary reason I loved it, but if you can have pleasure and food too, why not?

In the following pages I'll tell you of a young man's life on this river . . . my life. Perhaps you can share in the pleasure, adventure and discovery and understand the importance of the Penobscot River in my early life. Without the river, I can truly say I do not know where I would be today if I could not have escaped to it and to Mantawassuk, The Cove.

CHAPTER TWO

The Lay of the Land

TWO BEAUTIFUL EIGHT hundred foot hills in the southern portion of Holden, Maine give first life to the brook that provided solace and escape to me during the troubling times of my formative years. Johnson Brook first sees the light of day as ground water seeping from springs on the north sides of Copeland Hill and Rider Bluff. These two brooklets then converge in a wooded, boggy area after crossing Route 1a to the south of the Maine Central Railroad tracks. They are reinforced at this point by other waters flowing into them from bogs located at the bottom of Mann Hill.

These waters, filtered by the bogs and laden with nutrients, form the birthplace of Johnson Brook. The main brook now wanders slowly in a northerly direction and crosses under the Maine Central Railroad tracks and then meanders toward Eastern Avenue in Holden, Maine and on to its ultimate destiny with the Penobscot River and the sea. The brook's pace quickens as it nears and finally crosses under the avenue. This impatience is not rewarded, however, as the waters are slowed again and forced to traverse nearly two miles of flat, open farm country. Its volume is swelled again as it enters these fields by the confluence of another nameless brook entering it from the east. Its path is marked on its journey across this area by dense growths of alders and willows along its banks.

Here, near the Lambert Road, the brook enters the City of Brewer and it's there that it flows strongly into my life. Although I have walked its banks over nearly its entire course, this begins the section that is most familiar to me . . . its final two miles. To this day, I can close my eyes and still visualize every foot of it from the Lambert road to where it enters the Cove and marries with the Penobscot River.

After meandering through the farmlands and crossing under the wooden bridge on the Lambert Road, it is met again for the last time by yet another small brook from the east about a mile below the road. Together they rush impatiently over the ledges beneath electric power lines, commencing a drop in elevation of fifty feet in its final mile of life. This last mile I consider the most beautiful part of the brook. It rushes over a rocky bottom and runs through sweet smelling, high banked woods of pine, hemlock, cedar, spruce and fir; accented with stands of white and grey birch. Maple and the stately fan shaped elm; tower high and regally above all other growth. Large growths of several species of fern and wild iris grow among the moss-covered rocks along the banks, together with the broad leaves of the skunk cabbage, trout lilies and jack-in-the-pulpits.

Coming around its final bend, it nears its ultimate destination, the Penobscot River. But before it surrenders its waters to the anonymity of the river, the brook bestows one last gift to those of us that have wandered its banks and waded in its currents. Its waters pass under the small, concrete bridge on North Main Street in Brewer, ripples serenely over the rocks through an area of large willow trees, and then, finally; it spreads its cool waters out and mingles them with the still waters of the Cove.

Looking north across the Cove from the outlet of the brook, your eyes are met by a high bank, on top of which grows a large grove of white pines, shielding from view the river beyond. Near the center of the Cove, covered with maple trees, is a small, man made island no more than fifteen or twenty feet across.

The Cove spreads out to the left as you enter it from here, widening before turning to the right and into the river. Wild Irises, Common Cattails, Pickerelweed, Yellow Pond Lilies and Fragrant Water Lilies grow in the shallow waters on the south side to your left. The waters deepen beyond the island towards the river and patches of lily pads are scattered across its surface.

The waters are shallow where the brook first enters the Cove and flows by a long sand bar to the right. At the end of the sand bar, under the pine-covered bank, is a long, shallow appendix of the Cove. It circles around to the right and ends back near where the brook enters. In the spring of the year when the waters are high, the circle is complete and a large fern and maple covered island is formed to the right of the brook's inlet. We called this appendix the Little Cove. An aerial view seems to show that the Little Cove may have been, at one time in its past, the main course of Johnson Brook.

The Indians of this area must have felt something special in their hearts for the area of The Cove, also, for they put a name to it, Mantawassuk (manta-wah'-sook). Its meaning is, "inlet" or "at the mouth of". The name refers to The Cove only, and not to the brook entering it. Johnson Brook is called Eaton Brook on the maps of the area, but it has been known by other names in the distant past also; Nichols Stream, the Philips Mill Stream, or just "the brook" by all of us who lived near it. All we would have to say was we were going over to or down to, "the brook" and every one would know where we would be.

The Cove is not the same as it was before the arrival of the white man. The small island probably was not there, and the waters were not backed up into it from the dam in Bangor. I feel certain, however, that there had to have been a large pool at or near this spot, probably at the base of the pine-covered bank, before the brook made a sharp right turn and exited into the river.

Johnson Brook enters the eastern side of Penobscot about one and three quarters of a mile above the hydro-electric dam in Bangor, and about one and a quarter miles below the dam in Veazie, Maine. The entrance to The Cove and Johnson Brook is guarded on the down stream side by a gigantic, diamond shaped boulder framed by white birches and backed by tall, white pines. This twenty foot tall, pointed monolith is called, appropriately enough, Diamond Rock or Picked Diamond. Picked is probably a corruption of the word "picket" meaning sharp or pointed. This conspicuous landmark is not mentioned in the earliest history of the area, probably because trees masked its existence before the Bangor dam was built. The flooding of the area by this dam brought the waters of the Penobscot to the base of Diamond Rock and probably killed off those trees.

When my brother and I were young, nearly every fish that the state had to offer could be caught in the brook, The Cove or the river. They ranged from the lowly eel and hornpout (bullhead) to the elegant brook trout and to the gamest fish on the East Coast, the Atlantic Salmon, Pickerel, small mouth black bass, white perch, sunfish or sucker . . . all succumbed to our fishing skills, by hook or by crook; more about the "crook" part later.

The Cove and river fairly teemed with baitfish. Schools of golden shiners and other species of minnows seemed to be everywhere. The pickerel and bass gorged themselves and grew fat and heavy. Pickerel twenty inches long and longer were common. We invented our own special techniques for catching this finny bonanza whether they were biting or not.

Let me take you on a guided tour of our fishing grounds so you will be familiar with the spots I will be talking about later. We will leave The Cove and go up the river on its Eastern shore and return by going back down the river on the opposite shore.

As you leave The Cove and turn right, you are headed due east and are going upstream on the Penobscot River. A hundred yards or less upstream, a rocky ledge protrudes into the current far enough to disrupt the river's flow and a large eddy is formed. This is called Doughty's Landing, after the Charles Doughty family who owned this property. This is a good spot to fish for bass. Not too far above here is a sandy beach behind Emerson Dean's house. We would occasionally swim and wade here or have a picnic. The Simpsons, my family, lived in the next house above his.

A half-mile further upstream, the river veers sharply left from its easterly flow and comes from the north. At this point, you are leaving Brewer and are entering the Town of Eddington. This particular area is known as Eddington Bend because of this sharp turn in its course. This was the head of tide back in the days before this area was settled and the Bangor dam was constructed in 1876. It is believed to be here at Eddington Bend where Governor Pownal of the Massachusetts Bay Colony buried a leaden plate on the 23rd of May in the year 1759. Historians differ as to whether the plate was buried on the eastern side of the river or on the western side, but the consensus favors the height of land on the eastern side.

General Waldo, a grantee of the so called "Waldo Patent", accompanied Pownal on this trip to survey a grant of land, the limits of which encompassed the ground upon which he was standing, or so he thought. It is recorded he looked about and made the statement, "Here is my bound!" and then fell dead on the spot. You have to admire a man who knows his limits and will die for them.

After rounding the bend at this historic spot, the hydroelectric dam in the Town of Veazie comes into view. A concrete fishway through the dam on the eastern side of the river circumnavigates the dam at this point. The waters within the fishway are guided through a series of step-like catch basins, making it possible for fish to ascend the river to the waters above the dam. The top of the fishway is covered with a heavy, iron bound, wooden lattice work. If you lie on your belly, you can look through the lattice and sometimes see salmon working their way up the fish way.

Across the river is the powerhouse, a series of square, brick buildings squatting on massive concrete bases backed up against the hills in the Town of Veazie. You can almost feel the energy from the power lines as they cross the river directly over your head. The roar of the water as it passes over the dam and through the turbines makes it difficult to converse.

Crossing the river through the fast water below the dam brings us to the western side of the river and to the Town of Veazie. The waters are rocky and quick here until we get a few hundred yards down stream. The river's depth and width increases at this point and the river begins to slow somewhat. If you look to your right, there perched at the top of the hill with a beautiful view of Waldo's bound on the opposite shore, is a spot that is near and dear to my heart; the Veazie town dump. I remember this dump, warmly and fondly, as a combination antique store, shopping mall and recreation center of sorts.

Below the dump, the river is bounded on the west by a fifty or sixty foot high bank which drops sharply into the river all the way downstream and around the bend until you get to the electric sub-station directly across from the mouth of the Cove. Perched high atop these banks are many tall white pines. The bald eagles have their massive nests of sticks and twigs in some of them. It's a wonderful sight to see them soaring high above the river; eyes fastened to the waters below, watching for any good sized fish foolish enough to be near the surface while the eagle is hunting.

Sometimes they just sit in the tops of the trees and when their quarry is sighted they push themselves off their perch. With a few powerful pushes from their wings, they gather speed, rushing toward the surface of the river. Then, with a curious rocking motion, they snatch their meal from the waters; hardly getting their claws and talons wet.

I once saw an eagle grab what must have been a large salmon, as heavy as or heavier than itself. The waters exploded beneath its talons and the eagle was nearly pulled under. Somehow the eagle managed to get itself airborne once more and flew to the top of a tall pine, minus his dinner, near where Diamond Rock stabs at the sky. Perching on one of its topmost branches, he fluffed up his feathers and spread his wings to about half-mast.

Looking dejected and slightly embarrassed, he cast his eyes around the area, probably hoping no one had seen him bite off more than he could chew. After about fifteen minutes of drying his feathers in this cormorant-like pose, he took off and resumed his search for dinner, hopefully with slightly smaller aspirations. I could feel a certain amount of empathy for this particular bird because I had a similar experience to his not too many years previous. I'll tell you about it later.

Enough digression . . . let's cross the river now and return to The Cove. It's about two hundred yards across the river at this point and the river is comparatively deep. The river runs from east to west along here, so at times the westerly winds, blowing against the current, can cause the waters to be quite choppy. Entering The Cove, we are protected from the prevailing westerly breezes by the hill and tall pines behind Diamond Rock. It is nearly always serene here in The Cove.

We have now come full circle in my small fishing world. There are times when my brother and I have gone down the river and tried our luck at the Bangor dam, but these times were not too frequent. The river lacks character from below the Cove to the Bangor dam; it being mostly straight and deep without much good fishing until you are below the Bangor dam itself. The fishing is always more certain in the familiarity of The Cove and the Veazie dam area. As the saying goes, if you are already there, why leave?

Why, indeed? Now that I have familiarized you with this area, it is time for me to put on my thinking cap and try to haul up from deep within my mind as many incidents and happenings as I can that may be of interest to you. So, hang on to your hats; Memory Lane, here we come!

CHAPTER THREE

I'm Hooked!

MY FATHER CUT a long, slender alder from a group growing near the brook's edge. After trimming the branches from its length, he tied a piece of black, braided fishing line to its tip. The line was only a few inches longer than the pole, but that didn't matter. The little brook was no more than five or six feet across at its widest point. He tied the hook directly to the line and carefully threaded a squirming, pink earthworm over its sharp point.

"Watch this," he said, easing himself to the edge of the brook. He flipped the hooked worm through the sun-dappled shadows and it landed in the middle of the slowly moving waters. I watched the baited hook as best I could from my vantage point among the tall ferns.

The worm sank slowly from sight and was carried by the dark current toward a bend in the brook. The moment the worm reached the bend, the tip of the alder pole twitched. My father dropped the tip of the pole and let the trout run with the bait as far as it could with such a short line. Then, in one motion, he set the hook and flipped the trout through the air in my direction. Droplets of water sparkled in the sun as the trout sailed through the air and landed at my feet. It did a series of frantic flip-flops among the ferns and alders before finally lying still, its mouth slowly opening and closing as if gasping for air.

My father reached down and grasped the slippery fish behind its head and removed the hook from its mouth. Cutting a slender crotch from another nearby alder, he threaded one leg of the crotch through a gill cover of the trout and out its mouth.

"Here," he said, "You can carry this." He handed the stick with the trout on it to me. The moment the stick was in my hand, the trout started to wriggle furiously. Startled, I dropped it and moved away. My father laughed and said, "It can't hurt you. Pick it up and follow me."

I picked up the stick with the trout still attached and followed my father, looking at the fish occasionally and admiring its beautiful coloration. Brilliant red spots, surrounded by pale blue halos seemed to glow in contrast to the olive coloration of its sides and the dark, vermicular markings on its back. Lemons colored spots were scattered among the red ones, competing for my attention. This already beautiful display was accented by the orange-red blaze of its belly and the starkness of the black and white on the leading edges of its pectoral fins. I have caught many brook trout since then, but few have topped the beautiful coloration of that little native trout caught in a small brook in Levant, Maine when I was not yet five years old.

I have no recollection of the trip to that brook or of the ride home, but the catching of that particular fish seems to be burned indelibly into my memory and I hope it remains until the day I die. Whether or not my father caught any more trout that day does not matter. I was hooked on fishing from that day on; hooked as firmly as that little trout my father had caught. I am still hooked today, more than sixty years later.

The first fish I caught had none of the brilliance and appeal of a brook trout, but it was just as beautiful in its own way. It was a sunfish, a little pumpkinseed. I caught it one evening at Parks Pond in Clifton, Maine. My father had parked his Model "A" Ford just off Route 9 where Parks Pond grazes the edge the road. There was a small gravel beach at this spot and people sometimes stopped to picnic there.

My father wanted to fish for Pickerel, but they were not co-operating. Instead, he put a worm on the hook and handed the rod to me. I could see many fish swimming in the clear water over the gravel bottom. Some were darting almost to the shoreline. Most of them were shiners but there were a few sunfish there that were around three or four inches long. I didn't strip out any line or try to cast to them; I didn't know how. Instead, I dangled the line in the water a rod's length from shore. The shiners attacked the bait instantly but couldn't swallow it because the bait was too big for their mouths. One of the sunfish apparently thought the bait was a little too good for the likes of mere shiners, so it darted in and stole the worm from them. I lifted the rod tip and swung the tip towards shore. The sunfish was dangling from the end of the line; not because it was hooked, but because it was too stubborn too let go of the worm.

It fell from the line and landed on the beach. I tried to pick it up and learned a valuable lesson; spiny-finned fish can hurt you if you are not handled carefully. I wanted to keep it, but my father convinced me to toss it back into the pond so that, " . . . it could grow up." A three-inch sunfish doesn't provide one with much nourishment, and besides, a true Mainer would not be caught eating one under any circumstance. It did not matter. I was now a full fledged fisherman . . . a blooded warrior! I had caught my first fish!

I believe that it was about that time that things started to go wrong in my father's life, so I did not get to go fishing again for a few years. The urge must have been very strong in me, though, because whenever I would get near a body of water, be it frog pond or swamp, I checked it out to see if there were any fish in it.

I was fortunate to live where I did in North Brewer. Each day when I walked to school, I had to cross the bridge that went over Johnson Brook. We always stopped to toss rocks at any objects that may have been floating on its surface. It was great fun to drop a stick on the upstream side of the bridge and then quickly run across to the downstream side and make believe that we were bomber pilots. We used rocks and tried "bomb" the "ships" when they floated from under the bridge.

The fish were not safe from our bombardments, either. Nothing in the brook was sacred. We tossed rocks at them and they darted for cover under the bridge and stayed there until we left for school. I'm surprised they never learned to avoid open water when we kids were on our way to and from school. Tossing rocks at fish did not satisfy the urge nurturing in me since my first encounters with the world of fishing. I was determined to catch another fish. Not just any fish mind you, but a real one that you could eat. I finally settled on one of the Pickerel I had been observing from the top of the bridge over which I crossed each day. Pickerel held a fascination for me. Each day at the same time, the same fish would be in the same spot, facing in the same direction, usually under or near some lily pads. They hovered, looking like sleek submarines; pectoral fins fanning; maintaining their position and never moving a fraction of an inch. It was as if they were guarding their territory. They were constantly on the alert for prey or for any movement from above. If anything alarmed them, they scooted for deep water as if shot from a gun. Their flight is so swift you cannot follow it with your eyes. The only evidence showing a fish had occupied that spot was a boiling swirl of water where the fish had once been.

These consistent habits of pickerel can definitely be used to a fisherman's advantage. If you mess up on a certain fish today, he will be there the next day to give you another try at him, and the next day, and the next. Pickerel are; if nothing else, co-operative.

After deciding I just had to catch that certain Pickerel, a question had to be answered. How? I had no rod. My total experience in the fishing department had been watching one fish get caught by someone else, and catching but one myself; and it had been probably the most common fish the state had to offer. So, I asked around among my friends as to how I should go about catching my fish. No one seemed to know any more about fishing than I did, except one. He had a golden piece of information to offer. "You gotta ketch 'em with a spinner."

"What's a spinner?"

"It's a shiny round thing 'bout this big," he said, pointing at his thumbnail. "When you pull it through the water, it spins round and 'round. They think it's a sick fish. Pickerels only eat sick fish."

I vaguely recalled having seen something possibly answering that description tied to the line on my father's fishing rod. When I got home, I looked to see if what I remembered was indeed a spinner. Luck was with me. It seemed to be the very thing my friend had described. Attached to the wire shaft the spinner was on was a treble hook with red and white feathers tied in place and cut off square on the end.

Now the problem of a rod; or *lack* of a rod, came up. My father had forbidden me to use his rod unless he was there with me. Of course, he had not mentioned the spinner, so I guessed that it was all right to use that; and a piece of his line, too. But, what was I to use for a rod? Then I remembered that vision of me and my father on that trout brook and the Alder pole. There were no Alder poles near the bridge, but there were some long, straight, Cedar poles lying along side of the house that my mother had used for the pole beans one year. I could use one of those! I selected the one, which seemed to be the straightest and cut a piece of line from my father's rod and tied it to the end of the beanpole . . . with the spinner attached, of course. I looked proudly at my first fishing pole. So it was twelve feet long . . . so what? So it was two and a half inches in diameter at the butt . . . so what? With that contraption I could flip that spinner clear across the brook by the bridge. No Pickerel would find safe harbor from me and my killer outfit.

Balancing the rig on my right shoulder, I trudged the quarter mile down the road to the bridge. My heart was pounding as I looked over the concrete rail of the bridge. There he was, by God! Same time, same station! I figured I might need a little practice before the slaughter, so I crossed the road to the down stream side of the bridge and climbed down the embankment to the edge of the brook.

It then became obvious to me that my new outfit was just a little unwieldy. Each time I cast the spinner out into the brook, the heavy tip of the pole splashed into the water and the spinner went nowhere near my target. On my back casts, I nearly caught myself several times. I would have to develop a different technique of casting if I were to have a chance at my fish on the other side of the bridge. I soon found that by choking up on the pole a foot or so and flipping the spinner into the brook with an underhand motion, I could then manage a fairly respectable cast. I went through the motions a few more times and figured I was ready, so up the bank and across the road I went with my hefty rig.

I peered over the rail one more time to check on my fish. He was still there, totally unaware of his impending doom. All that commotion on the other side of the bridge had not fazed him in the slightest. I cautiously climbed down the bank on the opposite shore from my victim. My heart was pounding so hard that I was sure he could sense it. I positioned my feet as solidly as I could on the rocks. I couldn't see the fish from where I was, but I had carefully noted where he lay in relation to a big rock on the opposite shore.

The moment was at hand. I flipped the spinner across the brook to a spot near where the fish had been facing and started my retrieve. I dragged the lure all the way across the brook and nothing happened. I had fully expected the fish to smash the lure after it had gone only a few feet.

Overcoming my disappointment, I cast to the same spot once again. Once more the spinner approached my side of the brook with the same result . . . no strike. I began to think unkind thoughts about my friend who had recommended the spinner.

"Maybe the spinner isn't spinning," I thought. To check this out, I dropped the spinner into the water and dragged it a foot or two. Then suddenly it happened! My Pickerel shot up from the bottom; chomped onto the spinner and headed for the bottom again! I leaned into that beanpole and fifteen inches of Johnson Brook Pickerel went soaring through the air, headed for a crash landing somewhere on top of the bank near the road.

I dropped the pole and scrambled up the bank. The Pickerel didn't have time to flop more than twice before I was on top of him. I held the fish down until he stopped struggling. Sliding my hand to a spot behind his gills, I squeezed and lifted the fish up for a better look. The spinner was dangling from a corner of its jaw; the red and white fly concealed within its mouth. I forced its mouth open to see how well he had been hooked. It was then that I learned another valuable lesson. Pickerel have sharp teeth! Worse than that, Pickerel have *many* very sharp teeth!

That fish had somehow managed to grab the tip of my finger and was holding on for dear life. I yelled and shook loose from him, but not before I had donated some of my blood to the cause. I figured that to get him to give the spinner back would require a little persuasion, so I looked around for something to convince him of the error of his ways. I picked up a broken piece of tree branch and gave him a couple of persuasive blows on the top of his streamlined skull. This convinced him that I was the rightful owner of the spinner. He quivered a little and gave up the ghost. I pried his mouth open and learned my second valuable lesson of the day. It was that even *after* death; it could still be difficult to remove a firmly entrenched treble hook from the mouth of a Pickerel because those multitudes of teeth can *still* cut you up!

I finally extricated the hooks with a minimum loss of blood and pulled my pole to the top of the bank to join my fish and me. That was enough for one day. I shouldered my pole again, this time on the left side; my right shoulder was a little sore from carrying the pole to the brook. I slipped my right index finger into the gill cover of my quarry and started my proud march up the road to my house.

The tail of the fish occasionally dragged on the ground and gravel from the roadside stuck to its tail. It wasn't because the Pickerel was overly large; it was because I was rather small, being only eight or nine years old at the time and small for my age. I wonder what my mother must have thought as her son came through the door with cut and bloody fingers, holding up a dead Pickerel with a tail coated with roadside gravel, saying, "Will you cook it for me, Mama?" She must have gotten used to it, because it was a scene she was destined to live through many times over in the years following.

CHAPTER FOUR

By Hook or by Crook

I LEARNED AT an early age that baited hooks and lures are not the only methods a person can use to put fish on the table of a poor family. Other methods can be as effective or more effective, depending on conditions. One morning while walking to school, I surveyed the down stream side of Johnson Brook from the bridge on North Main Street. My eyes caught a slight movement in a small patch of lily pads at the water's edge. Could it be the current moving the weeds and grasses? The longer I looked, the more curious I became.

I warily made my way down the bank for a closer look. What I saw made my eyes bug out. Almost totally hidden by the weeds and lily pads, was a huge Pickerel! The motion, which had caught my eye, was one of his pectoral fins as it fanned the water, stabilizing his bulk as he hovered under the lily pads.

I could see only part of his head and one fin, but I knew he was much bigger than any Pickerel I had ever caught before. At once I started to think of how I could add him to my list of victims. Being on my way to school, I had no fishing rod with me, of course. I looked around for something else with which to do him in. He was only about four or five feet from shore and the water was about a foot deep where he was hovering.

I couldn't see anything that could be used as a spear, but my eyes caught sight of a fist size rock near my feet. Slowly I bent down to pick it up; keeping my eyes glued to the fish. Feeling around by my feet, my hand located the rock and my nervous fingers closed around its cold bulk. I started to ease myself up, but as I did, there was a violent surge in the water where the Pickerel had been. The water boiled and the lily pads twisted around as if in a maelstrom. Silt from the bottom clouded the water, and the fish was gone. I looked into the deeper water where I thought he may have gone, but he was nowhere to be seen. *Wow*, I thought, *what a fish!*

I clambered up the bank to the bridge and looked again, but there was no sign of him anywhere. Could my eyes have deceived me? Had there been a fish where I thought I had seen one? Maybe a muskrat had caused all that commotion. I headed for school with marvelous visions of this giant fish filling my young head.

I didn't tell any one about it. I didn't think they would believe me. Besides, if they did believe me, they might try to catch him before I did. Suddenly I felt very possessive of that fish. This was *my* fish . . . finders keepers!

By the next day I had almost convinced myself I had imagined the whole thing, but I thought I had better check out that patch of water lilies, anyway. I could see nothing from the bridge, but on an impulse, I picked up another rock and again eased my body cautiously down that bank toward the patch of water lilies.

Staying as low as I could, I sneaked up on the lily pads. My heart was pounding as I shaded my eyes and stared under the flat, round pads, looking for my fish. One of the pads made a slight motion, as if something had lightly bumped up against it. I concentrated my gaze under that pad and my heart skipped a beat. There he was! Deeper in the water than the day before, but he was real! He was not a world record, but he was more than big enough for me.

I knew he had seen me because his eyes were fastened on me and he was very slowly backing away from me, hoping that I had not seen him. He was trying to get to heavier cover nearer to the center of the lily patch. No time to waste, I thought. I threw the rock directly at his head with all the force I could muster! The water exploded skyward, lily pads were scattered apart and mud from the bottom slowly obscured my view with brown clouds of silt. The lily pads slowly drifted back together again after being displaced by the force of the rock I had thrown.

Again, as before, there was no sign of the fish. He had disappeared as completely as he had the day before. I was only mildly disappointed. I hadn't really expected to get him, I told myself. But, wouldn't it be something if I did get him; and with a rock? My primitive, cave man instincts were coming to the fore. The more I thought of it, the more the idea appealed to me. I looked about and gathered up a pile of fist sized rocks and laid them in a neat pile away from the water's edge. If he was there again the next day, I would be ready for him.

Mr. Pickerel was not there the next day, however, and I thought my rock throwing activities had scared him away for good. Maybe he had gone down stream and into The Cove. That did not seem too likely because the water was low and there was just a trickle flowing from the brook into the Cove. Maybe he had gone upstream. There seemed to be plenty of depth to the water in that direction. I hoped he hadn't because I really wanted to get that fish.

He wasn't there the next day, either, but the day after that proved my fears to be unfounded. He was back again and again I bombarded him with my cave man arsenal, but in vain. The results were the same; the big Pickerel vanished like a ghost and a disappointed boy trudged to school. This went on for several weeks and put a little excitement into my life. Each day I headed for the bridge for my rendezvous with the big pickerel. I was the great hunter, stalking his prey only to have the prey narrowly escape each time. It was a war of wits and the Pickerel seemed to have the upper hand. I hated to admit it to myself, but I could use a little help.

Help sometimes comes in strange ways. It came to me this time in the form of a Field and Stream magazine; or rather, an article in that magazine. The story that had caught my attention was about a man who caught large carp by shooting them with a bow and arrow with a line attached. The story stated that a fish is actually deeper in the water than he appears to be because of the refraction of the light rays as they come back out of the water. The bow fisherman said that you must aim below where the carp seemed to be in order to hit him.

Aha, I thought. *That's the answer! The Pickerel had escaped each time because the rock I threw at him was actually going over his back.* What a revelation! I had been shown the way and tomorrow I would try to make this valuable piece of information work for me.

The fateful day arrived and I was there early, primed with that valuable bit of information. I hoped it might possibly give me the necessary edge in this match of wits. I peered down from the bridge; very cautiously, as though I thought he might catch a glimpse of me even from that distance. Sure enough, there he was with his pointed nose protruding from under a lily pad. He hovered there, pectoral fins fanning the water and not suspecting a thing.

Again, down the bank I sneaked with a smooth, round boulder in my hand. I went farther around him this time, creeping up on him from behind, slow and low, scratching myself thoroughly in the process on some blackberry bushes that grew there. I tried to keep the lily pads between the fish's eyes and myself, hoping that he would not be able to see me until I could get a decent shot at him with my rock. I took the last few slow steps to the water's edge, rock raised and ready to throw. He didn't seem to suspect a thing. He was still hovering there, the lily pads between his eyes and me.

I took careful aim and let the rock fly! It hit the water right where I had aimed, just slightly below where his nose protruded from under the lily pad. Again, that now familiar explosion of water and mud, only this time I thought I had seen a momentary flash of white in the roiled waters as the commotion subsided. I peered down into the muddied waters and, there he was! His white belly was up and he lay motionless on his back on the bottom in the mud. I had done it! I had won! The Pickerel was mine!

Flushed with excitement, I looked around for something with which to retrieve my prize. I grabbed a dead tree branch and broke it into a hook shaped instrument and probed the muddy bottom, hooking at the fish and rolling it toward the shore. When I had maneuvered him close enough, I reached into the water and lifted him out for a closer look.

He was a good size fish; possibly weighing about two pounds. He was bigger than any I had ever caught before, but out of the water he did not seem to be as big as he had grown in my mind. I turned him over for a closer examination. My aim had been perfect. The rock had hit the fish dead center on the top of its skull. The skull had split grotesquely into a shattered mass. Eyes bulged from a head that was almost torn from its body. It was a sorry sight to behold. At that time I didn't know why, but my elation had been replaced by a sinking feeling in the pit of my stomach and my victory did not seem so great. I have since learned that the anticipation of an event can be much more exciting than the actual event.

I could not carry this shattered, pitiful carcass home to my mother and proudly ask her to cook it for me. I couldn't show it to anyone and exclaim, "Look what I caught!" The daily contest between boy and fish was over. There would be no more cautious, excited looks over the edge of the bridge . . . no more planning on how to outwit my fish. I had won . . . or had I?

I picked up my Pickerel's limp carcass and laid it carefully under the blackberry bushes that had punished me before, seemingly in anticipation of what I felt had become a misdeed. I headed for school, feeling strangely empty and sad. I had the same feeling I felt in later years when a friend had died, but this time I had done the killing.

That afternoon on my way home from school, I went down the bank to the edge of the brook one more time for a final look at my fish, but there was no sign of him. He was gone. He had disappeared again, this time for the last time. Had he ended up as a meal for a neighbor's cat; or more probably, a raccoon? I was glad that I had never told any of my friends about him. Never again was I to see a Pickerel as large as him in Johnson Brook.

CHAPTER FIVE

Sharks in the Cove!

A T THE MOUTH of Johnson Brook, just before the waters spread out into the deeper part of The Cove, was a large, flat rock. It was, perhaps, six or eight feet long by about half as wide and it angled out from the shore. It was not very large by adult standards, but it seemed to be the size of an aircraft carrier to me as a boy. You could get out to where it lay; about six feet from shore, by wading through a foot of water or, if you didn't want to get you feet wet, by jumping from rock to rock and hoping you didn't fall in.

It was an ideal spot to lie upon and observe aquatic life. The shallow, rocky bottom surrounding the rock gave shelter to many types of small fish such as minnows, sunfish, small bass and even a few tiny Yellow Perch and Pickerel. You could move any sizable rock and the chances were good that a small fish of some species would go darting away, looking for another place to hide from predators such as small, inquisitive boys. Under the end of the rock closest to shore, an overhang from the rock formed a shadowy cave. A few tiny sunfish and minnows or other varieties of small fish usually occupied this little haven.

It was fun to lie there on a warm, sunny day and drop a small portion of worm into the water and observe what fish would dart out of the cave and grab it. If you dropped two or three small pieces in a row, I found that you could then fool the fish if you dropped a tiny stone instead. The fish would dart and grab it, expecting it to be something edible. It would manipulate the stone in its mouth, finally spitting it out and head back under the rock to wait for something softer and better tasting.

Beyond the rock and about two-thirds of the way to the opposite shore, was the sand bar. When the water was low, the sand bar divided this part of The Cove into two sections. The water was much deeper beyond the sand bar; probably three or four feet deep in some places. The bottom there was not rocky, but instead, it was made up of gravel and sand. This was where the larger fish preferred to hang out. The sunfish built their round, shallow nests in the more shallow parts, but the bass and yellow perch dominated the deeper portions near the tree shaded bank of the opposite shore.

Muskrats had dug their burrows into this bank in various places, just below the water line. You could tell where these burrows were by careful observation of the muskrat. The muskrats would swim along the surface, usually trailing some choice pieces of vegetation from their mouths. About ten or fifteen feet from shore, the muskrat would dive beneath the surface. If you then watched very closely, you could see a fine stream of bubbles betray the muskrat's direction of travel. The bubbles would disappear at the shoreline, but no muskrat appeared on the shore. The reason he did not appear was because he had swum into the underwater entrance to his burrow. From there, the muskrat climbed up into his living chamber which was dug upward to above the water line, hidden inside the bank.

Sometimes an overly ambitious muskrat would enlarge his chamber to the point where the roof could no longer support its own weight and it would collapse. I remember walking along that bank once, trying to catch a large bass who kept jumping near a tree that hung out over the water. Just as I got to what I thought was the perfect spot for a cast to my fish, the ground gave way and my right leg paid a visit to a muskrat in one of those apartments. Needless to say, the commotion scared the bass away. I don't know what it did for the occupants of that chamber. Think of how you might feel if a gigantic foot as long as, or longer than, your own body came crashing through *your* roof. You might say, "There goes the neighborhood!" and move out.

It was on one of those beautiful summer days you read about in stories such as this, when the shark incident took place. Summer time in Maine usually has many days such as described, but the few that you really remember were usually accompanied by a memorable event which burned that particular day into your memory forever.

It had to have been late summer, probably late in July or early August. The waters of the Penobscot River and the Cove were lower than usual. When this happens, water temperatures rise, sometimes to seventy degrees Fahrenheit or higher in the shallow waters. Probably because of pollutants, large patches of green, hair-like algae had formed in the shallow waters surrounding the flat rock. I had made it out to the rock without getting my feet wet and was enjoying a newly discovered phenomenon. If you lie on your back and look straight up at the sky at the moving clouds with no trees or buildings within your peripheral vision, you could actually convince your mind you were the one moving through the sky at the speed of the wind.

This phenomenon can also be enjoyed by adults, but at the risk of you feeling a little foolish if caught. Young people, however, can enjoy this illusion most thoroughly at any time they please. It was fun to lie down in the middle of a field, or even on this hard rock, and imagine that you were on a magic carpet floating through the sky. Eventually, the inevitable finally happened and my magic carpet turned back into a hard, flat rock and I was forced to turn over and find a more comfortable position.

Back to reality again, I rolled over and cautiously peered over the side of the rock and into the little cave. To my fascination, an event was taking place that I would see repeated many times in the future, but never again so close to my eyes. The water was only ten or so inches deep and the flat rock was less than a foot above the water's surface, so I had the best seat in the house for the drama that was unfolding.

There in the warm waters directly below my eyes, was a small Pickerel about four inches log. His slender, pointed body was as stiff as a ramrod, but it was quivering as if charged with electric energy. His pectoral fins and tail fairly hummed as he moved himself ever so slowly through the water. He moved up and he moved down, sideways, backward and forward, stiff body never bending. Its movements reminded me of a hummingbird positioning itself in front of a flower in search of nectar.

I wondered what this display was all about. Then I noticed that his large, saucer shaped eyes were always staring in one direction. No matter where his nervous fins positioned that rigid little body, his eyes were fixed in only one direction. Following his gaze, I saw the object of his hypnotic stare. A small group of shiners was nonchalantly going about their own business, totally unaware of being observed from above by me and below by this quivering, wide-eyed fish.

He seemed to have homed in on one specimen in particular, a shiner nearly as long as he was. No matter where this shiner would move, Mr. Pickerel's pointed snout was aimed right at him, as if locked on by some mysterious radar. As the moments passed, the two fish gradually drew closer together.

Then it happened! The only thing my eyes detected was a small cloud of tiny silver scales scattering in the water. I had seen no movement from the Pickerel that would have indicated he was ready to strike. He was there one moment and in the next he was occupying the same space as the shiner; nearly a foot from where he had begun his strike, and I had not seen him move! I learned then what the expression, "in the blink of an eye" really meant.

The tiny Pickerel had caught the shiner just behind its gills and it protruded from both sides of his mouth. The Pickerel chomped on the shiner several times as if trying for a better grip with its sharp teeth. After a few moments, satisfied that its prey would not escape, the Pickerel slowly moved to the deeper water at the edge of the flat rock and stopped in its shadow. He acted as if he were a thief and did not want anyone to see what he had stolen.

Then he began the chore of trying to swallow his dinner. I say chore, because he seemed to be having quite a time of it. As I said before, the shiner was nearly as long as the Pickerel himself. With quick little chomps and jerks of his head, he gradually maneuvered the shiner around until only its head was in his mouth; tail and body pointing out.

Then he proceeded to swallow his victim. Again, with those quick little chomps, the shiner began to disappear on a one way trip into the Pickerel's gullet. With each chomp, the shiner's silver scales glittered and littered the water around the Pickerel's head. Some even squirted through his gills, scraped off by his sharp teeth.

At last, the inevitable happened. The shiner bottomed out in the Pickerel's stomach. The little Pickerel could force his dinner in no farther. There was one small catch, however. There was still a good half-inch or more of the shiner's tail protruding from the Pickerel's mouth! This didn't seem to bother him very much. He just settled back into the shade of the cave a little farther in and closer to the bottom; apparently resigned to the fact that he would have to wait a while before he could hunt again.

During my close-up observation of this spectacular piece of gluttony, I had gradually worked my head farther over the edge of the rock to keep the Pickerel in view. By now my chin was only a few inches over the surface of the water.

Suddenly, the Pickerel seemed to decide this may not be the best place to digest his dinner after all, and rapidly swam deeper into the cave under the rock. I thought I had moved my head too fast and that caused him to leave, but that turned out not to be the reason at all. In seconds it became obvious why he had departed so suddenly. There, literally under my nose in the warm, shallow water, appeared a fish so large that I could not believe my eyes! I froze and could not move. It seemed as if the fish would never stop going by my face! His body was so large that his back, dorsal fin, and the top of his tail were protruding from the water!

After he had finally swum by my face, I quickly rolled to the safety of the middle part of my rock and stood up, very scared! In my young mind, the only fish I knew of that swam with its fin out of the water was a shark! Never mind that this was fresh water and I was in a river miles from the ocean, my mind screamed, "Shark!"

Standing there in the middle of my haven, I looked about. There were "sharks" everywhere! The one who had passed under my nose was the biggest of the bunch and seemed to be the leader of the pack. Wherever he swam, the others followed. They swam in large circles among the rocks and algae. One edge of the circle went right by the edge of the rock where I was standing. The sand bar prevented them access to the deeper water beyond and the water was too shallow and rocky for them to swim up the brook.

The leader was a sight to behold. His girth was so great that his back or dorsal fin was almost always protruding from the water. In the shallower waters, he actually had to lie over on his side and beat the water frantically with his tail to make any progress. Some of the others were very large, also. Their dorsal fins cut through the shallow water too, but not as much as the leader.

They must have entered this part of The Cove at the spot where the brook had cut a slightly deeper channel close to the shore next to the flat rock on which I was standing. This channel goes from the rock and follows the shore around the Point where The Cove becomes deeper and empties out into the river. They had probably been attracted to this spot because of the cooler waters of Johnson Brook flowing into The Cove. The "sharks" didn't seem to be able to find their way out through the narrow channel they had come through and they just kept circling and circling.

There were so many I couldn't count them all, but I'm certain there must have been at least two dozen of them. They swam and splashed around me for a while and then one of them found the opening leading to the deeper water. As if the information had been passed on to all of them, the parade of fish disappeared with him into the deeper waters of The Cove. I leaped from the flat rock towards the shore, getting both feet thoroughly wet in the process and clambered up the bank to "safety." I did not want to be on that rock if they ever came back.

In later years with more fishing experiences under my belt, I learned they were not sharks at all, but instead were the king of fresh water fish, the Atlantic Salmon. I realized also, that if indeed a thirty pound Atlantic Salmon had ever swum up the Penobscot River and entered The Cove, he had done so that day; and only inches from my nose!

CHAPTER SIX

The Day of the Eagles

IT'S A TRUISM that all journeys start with a single step. For me, that single step was usually the one I took from the back porch of my house and onto a pathway behind our house. It led eventually to the river or to The Cove. I could more easily reach The Cove by walking out the front door and walking down North Main Street to Johnson Brook and then to The Cove. It was always more fun, though, and had more potential for adventure, if I started my little journeys by way of the path behind the house.

This path began near the base of a tall spruce tree of about eighteen inches in diameter. Fifteen or twenty feet beyond the spruce, the path went beneath a wild apple tree. It was sometimes loaded with small, yellow apples about two inches in diameter and of questionable heritage. After the frosts in early fall, the ones left on the tree took on a sweetness and were somewhat palatable.

A few yards beyond the apple tree, the path reached the edge of the woods that grew between the river and our house. Here in the woods, it made a sharp left turn and ran parallel to the river, which was now only about two hundred feet away. These woods were made up of a variety of evergreens such as cedar, spruce, and fir, but these trees were dominated by many tall white pines.

Several of these tall pines were on the property line of our neighbor, Emerson Dean. Here they served double duty as possibly the tallest fence posts in North Brewer. A fence made up of two strands of barbed wire enclosed Mr. Dean's back pasture area and in places, these strands of wire were nailed firmly to the bases of these pines. They had been in place for so long the trees had actually grown around the wire in several places.

My brother, Trevor, and I had spiked some small pieces of boards to one of these pines and used them as a ladder to reach its lower branches. Once these branches were reached, we could then climb almost to the top of this particular tree. We had built a tree house of sorts out of a few heavy, pine planks that we nailed to some branches about three-quarters of the way up the tree. The view from there enabled us to see across the river and as far downstream as Mount Hope Cemetery in Bangor. After the leaves had fallen in autumn, you could see the eagle nests in the tall pines across the Penobscot.

Once lightning struck our pine tree. It punched a fist size hole through one of the boards of our platform and stripped a piece of bark off the western side of the tree all the way to the ground. Lightning can give you a very convincing demonstration of its power. I have seen trees looking as if they had been blown apart by high explosives after a lightning hit. I was a little leery of the platform after that, even though it has been said lightning never strikes twice in the same place. I thought I would like to put that particular theory to a test by putting who ever dreamed it up, in this pine tree during the next thunderstorm.

Beyond the pines and the fence, this path connected to another pathway that came from Mr. Dean's house and led directly to the river. At this point I had to choose between following the other path to the river or cutting across Mr. Dean's pasture and walking to the cove by way of Charles Doughty's back field.

If the water level was low, I would usually go down Mr. Dean's path and follow the river's shore downstream to the Cove. There were a few sweet crabapple trees along this path, and if it were late enough in the year, I would load up my pockets with these sweet little offerings to munch on as I was walking along.

At one time, Mr. Dean's shorefront had one of the few sandy beaches along this part of the river. When we were very young, my mother would occasionally take us on a picnic at this spot. There are a few rocks large enough to sit on by the shore. One time she had finished smoking a cigarette while on the biggest of these rocks. She flipped the cigarette butt out into the river about six feet from shore. Suddenly the water exploded where the butt had hit. A huge small mouth bass, thinking it to be food, struck it with a vengeance! We all were awe struck and I remember asking her if the fish had burnt its lips.

Even more certain than death and taxes is the following fact. Put a boy near a body of water and he is certain to start looking for rocks and will start throwing them into it. When I stop and think about it, I must come to the conclusion that a great deal of my younger life was spent throwing stones and other objects into bodies of water of one kind or another. Whether it was dropping hefty rocks from the bridge over Johnson Brook onto "enemy ships" floating downstream in the brook, or just seeing who could throw a rock farthest out into the Penobscot River, rock throwing seems to have been one of my major diversions in my younger days.

On "the day of the eagles", I was walking down the shore of the river on my way to the Cove. I was honing my rock throwing skills to as fine an edge as possible. It was one of those days a champion rock thrower would have to classify as ideal. It was hot and muggy and the river's surface was not marred by even the hint of a breeze. I was playing at one of the rock throwing games I invented and enjoyed the most. One was called "dive bombing" and the other was "torpedoing'.

In "dive bombing", the object of the sport was to see how close you might come to something floating in the water by throwing a stone high into the air and letting it drop as near to vertical as possible into the water. The chances of hitting your target in this sport were almost zero, but a near miss is very satisfying. It's more fun if you have a partner in this game. The one who comes closest in three throws is the winner. These were my rules. You can make up your own.

If you pick the proper stone; one that is smooth and as close to being round as possible, and if the stone is thrown nearly straight up, it will enter the water with hardly a splash. This is always a good way to tell if you have made a good "dive bomber" throw. Even with your eyes closed, the rewarding "ka-plug" sound as the stone hits the water will tell if you have made a good throw.

One time I made the mistake of throwing a stone nearly straight up and into the noonday sun. Nearly blinded, I waited for the familiar "ka-plug" sound of the stone hitting the water, but was rewarded instead with "ka-plotch". The stone buried itself into the wet sand only inches from my toes. Being a quick learner, I was always careful afterwards to not make the *ultimate* "dive Bomber" throw; that being straight up and then straight down onto the top of my head!

"Torpedoing" is a much safer throwing game and much more visually satisfying. The target can be anything that floats; stick, bottle, can, seagull . . . swimmer! You then find a flat, round rock and with a low, sidearm motion, the rock is sent skimming and skipping over the water's surface toward the target.

This sport is best performed on a day such as described above. A smooth surface is requisite as a wind chopped surface will cause the stone to skip erratically and good accuracy is nearly impossible. I had found an empty whisky bottle and had thrown it out into the river's current. As the bottle floated lazily downstream in the sluggish current, I kept pace with it as I walked along the shore.

I picked up flat rocks and tried to hit the bottle, skipping the stones across the smooth surface. At times the rock would skitter to a stop and sink before it reached the bottle. At other times the rocks would hit the surface and go flying in other directions as if they had a mind of their own. This was usually caused by not being able to find the perfect stone. Imperfections in their surfaces can cause erratic flight. Finally, as I neared Doughty's landing, all variables jelled and a nearly perfect flat, round stone skittered across the surface and neatly cut the neck off the bottle and it sank beneath the surface with a satisfying gurgle; another "enemy ship" down the drain.

With this accomplishment under my belt and my self esteem inflated a few notches, I continued past the landing and looked for another target. My reverie was rudely shattered by what sounded like a loud piercing scream. I looked around for the source of the eerie sound that had made the hair on the back of my neck stand at attention, but I saw nothing. Then I thought that maybe one of my friends was playing a joke on me, so I tried to appear nonchalant and started to walk again.

Then the screaming started again! This time it was not a single scream, but obviously several screams from more than one source. I realized then that it was not a joke and that the source of those hair-raising shrieks and whistles was in The Cove near the mouth of Johnson Brook. I was not sure what I would see as I clambered up the riverbank and into the coolness of the pine grove. I ran the short distance through the pines and scurried down the bank opposite the mouth of the brook.

As I got to the bottom of the embankment, something splashed heavily into the shallow, rock filled waters near the flat rock at the mouth of the brook. Seconds later, a huge, feathered form dropped out of the skies and hit the water at the same spot. Beating its huge wings frantically, it rose from the water. Clutched in its sharp talons, was an extremely large, squirming eel. The snow-white head of this bird betrayed its identity immediately.

A Bald Eagle, I thought excitedly, *what a sight!*

The great bird with its heavy load had not risen more than fifty feet into the air when the screaming began again. From above, another eagle swooped down on him. Piercing shrieks filled the air as the first eagle dropped the eel in an effort to defend itself. The eel hit the water once more and it seemed as if suddenly the hot, dead air was full of noisy, screaming eagles! They seemed to be everywhere!

Diving, swooping, screaming; they all tried to get this seemingly easy meal as the eel in turn tried to make it to the shelter of the willow trees that lined the entrance to the brook. The taloned onslaught continued, but no sooner would one eagle get airborne with the unfortunate eel than another one would attempt to steal it from him. I had a front row seat to the nature show of a lifetime!

I had seen these eagles many times before. Eagles were a common sight along this part of the river, nesting as they did in the pines on the north side of the river. I had heard their sounds and had seen them fishing countless times before. I had also seen how adept they could be at hijacking a meal from an osprey. They swooped down at the unsuspecting fish hawk and would scare him into dropping its prey. Sometimes the huge eagle could catch the hijacked fish before it hit the water.

But these had been sights seen from a distance. Now I was in the midst of it with swooping, screaming eagles sometimes only a few feet away, raising the hair on the back of my neck and causing goose bumps on my arms. They were everywhere, all intent on catching the same eel for lunch. I counted seven eagles for sure, but I could not be certain there were not more.

Then I saw a neighbor running towards the commotion on the other side of the Cove. I saw that he had a rifle in his hands. I yelled at him not to shoot, that it was only eagles causing the ruckus. He stopped at the Point and looked at the wheeling, swooping noisemakers. He shouted back, "Don't worry! I'm not going to shoot! I wasn't sure what in hell was going on down here. That's one hell of a sight, isn't it?"

The eagles must have decided that either the meal wasn't worth the hassle or there was one human being too many around there, and as suddenly as they had appeared, they were gone. The neighbor slowly shook his head and went back up the path to his house. With him and the birds gone, silence descended on the Cove.

I hurried around the Cove as quickly as I could to get to the mouth of the brook. The eagles never did get the big eel. I had seen him swimming through the green algae and rocks, moving up the brook toward the bridge. He wasn't at the mouth of the brook when I got there, but I caught up with him near the spot where the brook widens and deepens just below the bridge.

The eel was indeed a large one. It looked to be more than a yard long. In spite of being airborne several times in the sharp talons of several eagles, he seemed to be none the worse for his experience. I could see only two or three spots on his body that looked as if the talons had penetrated. Standing on a rock, I watched as the snake-like fish oozed over the final rocky obstacle. Then, its undulating body slowly disappeared into the deeper, shaded waters below the bridge. Its slime covered tough skin and extremely flexible body had saved him from ending up as a meal for one of the seven eagles.

I hadn't seen that many eagles in one spot before and haven't since. There are spots in the United States where it is possible to see that many or even more at one time, I suppose, but here in Maine those days may be gone forever. I can count myself as among the lucky to have experienced such a sight and from such a close proximity. To this day I can still hear and feel the intensity and excitement of that too brief moment in my life.

CHAPTER SEVEN

The Urge to Float

I CAN'T IMAGINE that there are a lot of advantages to being reared in poverty, but poverty does have *one* very important advantage; it forces you to use your mind. When you are young, inexperienced and have no training for anything in particular but do have an inquiring mind, you can find solutions to problems that are ingenious if nothing else. So it was with my brother Trevor and me.

After a few years of fishing along the river shore and the shores of The Cove, it became obvious to us that we were missing a lot fishing action by not being able to go out onto the waters that lay beyond our best casts. We could see all that piscatorial drama taking place out there among the lily pads just beyond our reach. The big Pickerel were out there among those pads in the waters that were too deep to wade and too far away to be reached by our longest casts.

It was sheer torture for a young fisherman to see a school of minnows suddenly scoot away from danger way out there on the edges of those pads as a large Pickerel or bass would pick off one of their number for a snack. The schools of minnows sounded as if a thousand tiny pebbles had hit the water at the same time as they fled from their common danger.

They didn't always flee from only Pickerel or bass. The Belted Kingfishers never had to work very hard for a meal, either. With plentiful meals swarming only an inch or two under the surface, there were always plenty of those noisy, chattering birds around. All it would take was the shadow of a bird passing through the minnow schools to spook them. Anything that was perceived by them to be a danger caused them to depart as one in noisy, liquid swooshes.

The obvious solution to our problem was, of course, a boat. But we had no boat and those neighbors that did have them were not too anxious to lend them to young, inexperienced sailors such as my brother and me. Needless to say, I was primed and ready to go when one day Trevor came home and said to me, "Let's go fishing. I built a raft."

No one has ever had to ask me more than once to go fishing with them, but the thought of being able to get out to the hot spots I had observed from shore was an added incentive. It gave added speed to my steps as we headed down North Main Street to The Cove. He had anchored the raft at the tip of the Point where the brook enters The Cove. I didn't quite know what to expect as we went down the brook to the Point, but when we finally arrived and I caught sight of his raft, my heightened spirits dropped back to earth so hard that you could almost hear the thump. A graduate of the Thor Heyerdahl School of Raft Building had definitely not built the raft. Kon Tiki it was not.

"Have you been out on this thing yet?" I asked, trying to mask my apprehensions with a show of nonchalance.

"Sure," he said proudly, "I've been all over The Cove with it. Come on. Let's go fishing."

The confidence in his voice shoved my fear into the background for the moment. With fishing rod in hand, I stepped toward that thing in the water, common sense giving way to my urge to fish.

The raft had been pieced together from various pieces of flotsam and jetsam that had been stranded in The Cove from years of floods and freshets. The more solid parts were four-foot pieces of old pulp logs, but the rest of his craft was made up from parts of other timbers and various weathered boards of uncertain origin. A rusty hinge on part of an old door decorated one of the boards that held the raft together.

The raft was anchored to the shore not with an anchor, but with a long alder pole jammed through one of the numerous holes in the raft's floor, if you could call it that, and stuck into the gravel bottom of The Cove. Trevor jumped confidently on board and pulled the pole out of gravel bottom and up through the bottom of the raft. He pushed the raft free so that it floated a couple of feet from shore. "Hop on," he cried.

I jumped onto the raft, which was only five or six feet square, landing next to my brother. The side of the raft on which we were standing began to sink slowly beneath the surface of the water and the other side began to rise ominously in slow motion. The raft was about to tip and dump both of us into the water and end our adventure before it began. Quickly, I hotfooted over to the slowly rising side of the raft and the vessel began to regain equilibrium once more. The floorboards were still awash and nearly even with the surface of the water. If either of us had weighed ten pounds more, I was convinced the raft would have settled to the bottom. Trevor gave a long, slow push on the pole and the raft moved slowly out into the deeper waters and towards those tantalizing groups of lily pads.

After we got out to the deeper water, I began to think about the fact that I didn't know how to swim and I wasn't sure if Trevor knew how to, either. If either of us moved around at all, the other had to move to a corresponding spot on the other side of the raft to prevent it from tipping. After floating around for a while, we learned to balance the precarious vessel almost automatically. You could sense it settling to one side or the other and you would shift your weight accordingly to strike a balance.

We survived that first voyage with no casualties after enjoying some good fishing that day. Rafts that we built later were larger and more stable. One of them even had a live box to keep our fish alive until we were ready to go home. The box was merely a rough wooden frame with chicken wire covering it and was hung over the edge of the raft in the water.

Rafts of the proper size can provide an excellent fishing platform, but they all have some drawbacks. A raft built early in the year from dry wood will absorb enough water by midsummer to cause it to sink if too large a load is put on it, so you might have to add more dry logs to it as the summer wears on. They are too large and heavy to pull up on shore to dry out after each outing. Another problem was that you could not go out on the river with it because the pole could not reach bottom. It would be a difficult problem for fledgling builders to rig up one of these rafts for rowing.

Whenever I think of rafts, I am embarrassed when I remind myself of *my* first attempt at raft building. One spring day just after the ice had left The Cove, I discovered a large tree felled by the March winds lying there parallel to the shore of the Little Cove. It was a foot or more in diameter and at least forty feet long and very straight. It had been blown down only a few feet from the shoreline. When my eyes first spotted it, the thought of a raft leaped immediately into my mind. I was to learn that a tree of that size could be more than a match for a young boy.

I ran home and returned with a bucksaw, axe, hammer and some nails and set to work on the fallen tree. I don't recommend this procedure to anyone wanting to build a raft. After several days of hacking and sawing, I managed to force the tree to give up a half dozen five or six foot logs. The tree, in return, had forced me to give up a little blood and a lot of sweat and blisters. It had also given me more sore muscles than I thought a body of my size possessed.

I levered the logs together one by one until I finally had them laid side by side and pointed toward the water. I then fastened them into a solid unit by spiking several boards across them. I had tied a large rock to the end of a piece of old clothes line and was going to use it as an anchor. It was placed in the middle of my craft. The other end of the rope was tied firmly to the raft. At last, after much effort, the raft was ready to launch. I thought it was the most beautiful thing I had ever seen. I could picture myself on board it, poling it around The Cove; captain of my own ship . . . the Tom Sawyer of the Penobscot. I was nearly quivering with anticipation.

Now, at last, the job of launching it into the waters of The Cove was upon me. I tried pushing, kicking and finally cursing it, but all in vain. There was not a curse horrendous enough or embarrassing enough that would make that pile of logs move an inch. It would not budge. All of my strength and effort brought it not an inch closer to the water. It just lay there, only a few feet from the water, teasing me. I attacked it again, using poles as levers but the poles broke and the raft stayed where it was, seemingly cemented to the ground. If inanimate objects could laugh, this one would have been in a fit of hysteria!

Being a true Mainer, I don't give up easily. I did not give up on this project either. I just became more stubborn about getting that damned raft into the water. I had noticed that when I tried to lever the raft into the water, I could raise one corner of the raft a few inches from the ground before the pole broke.

That's it, I thought! *I'll raise it up a little at a time and block it up with rocks.*

After that, I could push round poles under it and use them as rollers. Pure genius! I had just invented the wheel!

I jacked the front end of it up an inch or so at a time, sliding rocks and sticks under it to keep it from settling back into the soggy ground. After what seemed like hours, the leading edge of the raft was finally about a foot off the ground. Another great victory for the Simpson kid!

I then cut down a birch tree of about three or four inches in diameter and sawed it into lengths long enough to reach across the breadth of the raft. I slid them beneath the raft and parallel to the shoreline. I put three or four of these white rollers under it. I then knocked the rocks and sticks out from under the raft and it settled down solidly onto the rollers. I half expected the raft to roll into the water all by itself, but stubborn to the end, it did not. It still sat there, stolid and unyielding; but I thought I could detect a hint of fear in it now. It was beginning to learn who its master was.

I cleared all the sticks and stones from in front of it, making sure that there were no obstacles in its path. Nothing would stop it now. I could almost taste the victory. Relief was just a push away! To be on the safe side, I cut down another birch tree and sawed it up into a few more rollers to place in the path of this recalcitrant monster to insure its passage into the waters of the Little Cove.

At last, all preparations were complete and I stepped back and surveyed the results of my efforts. I felt confident there was nothing that could keep me from cruising on the waters of the Cove before the day was finished. I was somewhat battered and bruised, but when you are young, whatever you lack in brains and experience is more than made up for by a natural resiliency of body and spirit.

The big moment was now at hand. Sitting on the ground behind the raft, I placed both feet on its stubborn backside. With all my remaining strength I pushed with both legs as hard as I could. Very slowly the raft began to move. I maintained the pressure and the raft kept moving toward the water. It was working! I was in ecstasy! With a final burst of strength, I added impetus to the rolling mass of logs, spikes and rock anchor and the raft slid silently out into the water, defeated at last. It lethargically floated out into the water about ten feet and then the impossible happened! It slowly . . . *very slowly*, began to sink! I couldn't believe what my eyes were telling me! My wooden raft had sunk to the muddy bottom of the Little Cove.

I sat there, struck dumb! I still couldn't believe it! A raft made of wooden logs had just sunk to the bottom of the Little Cove in front of my very own eyes! The impossible seemed to have happened. Wood was not supposed to sink, it was supposed to *float*. At least, that is what I had always thought. What I didn't realize, and what a forester told me in later years, was that I had probably cut up a maple tree. In the spring of the year, the maple is saturated with moisture and its already dense, heavy wood is heavier still. Apparently, all this additional moisture coupled with the additional weight of spikes and nails and the rock anchor, was enough to take my hard-earned raft to the bottom of the Little Cove. I had won my battle and but had lost my war.

Building a lead raft was not my only ship building accomplishment. A few years later, I invented the corrugated cardboard punt. This was another bit of inventive genius born of the same frustration which had spawned the lead raft. It seems that as soon as man overcomes one problem, another awaits in a never ending cycle. Rafts had freed me from the limitations of fishing from the shore but had not freed me from the restriction of The Cove itself. There was a large river out there with more adventure waiting, but it could not be explored with a tiny raft. What I needed desperately was a boat. I had no boat, of course, nor the money or materials to buy or build one. These handicaps would possibly have discouraged one with less mettle than mine. Instead, I put on my thinking cap and tried to come up with a solution that could be accomplished within my extremely limited means.

One day I was idly playing with a piece of waxed paper in our kitchen. I folded the paper into the shape of a tiny canoe. I welded the ends of the canoe together by heating them over the wood stove and holding them together with my fingers until the wax cooled and bonded the paper together. I put the little canoe into the water bucket by the sink and watched it float about, wishing that I were only an inch tall so I could get in it and do some exploring.

Wouldn't it be great, I thought, *if I had some waxed paper big enough and strong enough to build my own canoe?*

That was silly! I knew that waxed paper didn't come in sheets that big or that heavy. Still, wouldn't it be great if it did? Maybe, I thought again, I could make my own waxed paper. But how? You can't get ordinary paper that large or that heavy, either. Now my thinking was taking on a life of its own.

My gaze lighted upon a cardboard box in the corner of the kitchen. Inspiration struck! What is cardboard? It's heavy paper, of course! But then again, what it is not? It is not heavy *waxed* paper. It would not be of much use to me unless I could some how turn it into waxed paper. But, again, how?

Inspiration, unlike lightning, can strike twice in the same place. I suddenly remembered a method that one of my teachers had used to preserve the beauty of the autumn leaves of this area. She had melted paraffin wax until it smoked and we had dipped the leaves into the melted wax for a few seconds. The hot wax had penetrated the surface of the leaves and their beauty was preserved for a few months more than they would have without the protective coating. *This* was how I could wax the cardboard and render it waterproof.

There would be no problem coming up with enough cardboard for the job, but I didn't have access to the amount of wax that I would need. I scoured the house for candles and sealing wax, but it did not yield up enough to coat even a single box. I then made the rounds of my friends' homes, and on the pretense that my mother needed some wax for canning, I accumulated an amount that I felt was sufficient for the job.

Early one bright, sunny day, I carried all the materials that I thought I would need down to the sandy shore behind Mr. Dean's house. I took the wax, cardboard boxes, nails, tacks, staples; a few boards to use as seats, some cedar laths, an old paint brush, a coffee can to melt the wax in and some matches.

I managed to construct a frame of sorts about six or seven feet long by three feet wide and a foot or so deep. The ends of this rectangular frame slanted in from the top of the bow and stern, giving the sides a trapezoidal shape. I tacked, nailed and stapled the corrugated cardboard from the boxes to this rickety framework. This seemed to add some rigidity to the craft. The seat was nothing more than a board nailed across the gunwales slightly behind mid ship. And then came the piece de resistance . . . the bit of genius that would make this whole idea work . . . the wax!

I built a small fire on the shore and melted the candles and paraffin sealing wax in the old coffee can. After the wax was melted and smoking, I turned my new boat over on its back and applied the smoking wax to its bottom and sides until there was none left.

The moment that I had waited for finally was there. Would the boat leak or not? Turning it back over, I carefully slid it over the sandy beach and eased it into the water. I inspected it with great care, half expecting to see little geysers of Penobscot River water squirting up through the bottom, but . . . wonder of wonders; there were none! Not a single spurt! It did not leak.

It was obvious to me the bottom of my new boat would not tolerate the weight of a person, even one as small as myself. I solved that problem by laying a few boards lengthways on its bottom to spread my weight around and to prevent my feet from breaking through. I didn't have a paddle, so a narrow board was drafted into service to fill that need. I stepped into the little craft, settled into place on the seat and pushed the boat free of the shore with my "paddle".

I was timid at first and stayed close to the shore. I paddled up the river near where the Grange Hall is located. Then I turned around and paddled back. I had grown a little braver now and decided to take a little trip down to The Cove. After that, who knows? A trip up to the Veazie dam, maybe.

On the way down to The Cove, just before reaching the eddy beyond Doughty's landing, the side of my craft brushed against the rocks that protrude out into the river at that point. I had cut in too close to the rocks and the current forced me against them. I thought nothing of it, just a slight bump, nothing to worry about. That slight bump turned out to be the kiss of death, however, and before I reached The Cove, water was seeping in where the wax coating had been scraped away.

By the time I managed to get the boat ashore halfway to the mouth of The Cove, the bottom of my boat was a soggy brown mess. After taking the floorboards out, I could see there was no sense in trying to repair it. I could punch my fingers through the bottom with no effort at all.

I was disappointed and disgusted at the same time. It seemed to me that I would never realize my dream of being able to go wherever I wanted to go on the river. I decided to salvage some pleasure from my misfortune anyway, so I waded beside it and pulled my soggy boat back up the river to Doughty's landing where the rocks had put an end to my career as a river boat captain. Pointing it out into the current, I gave it a shove. A few feet from shore, the current caught it and it swung around and it slowly headed downstream.

I followed it along until I got to The Cove and engaged in my dive bombing and torpedoing games, using it as my target. It was very easy to hit an enemy ship that size and my short-lived boat was sitting extremely low in the water with many holes showing as it finally drifted out of range down the Penobscot.

I didn't let my disappointment bother me too much. As I walked back home along the river shore I was already thinking. *Hm-mm*, I thought, *I wonder if I can build a boat out of tarred paper and seal it with roofing tar.*

CHAPTER EIGHT

Everything You Wanted to Know About Pickerel

ALTHOUGH, AS PREVIOUSLY mentioned, there were many species of fish in The Cove upon which to test your piscatorial skills, the number one species for Trevor and me was the Pickerel. He was number one with us for several reasons. First, he was plentiful. The Pickerel was the most dominant large fish in the Cove and he could be caught nearly anywhere within its boundaries. Another reason for his popularity with me was this. I could catch him with just about any kind of bait or lure. He wasn't shy and attacked with equal vigor, live bait, dead bait, worms, flies, streamers, spinners, spoons, plugs or just about anything else that you cared to throw at him that would fit in his mouth; or maybe *not* fit in it.

But, the topper to all this is, he can really fight if given a fair chance on the proper tackle. If these were not enough reasons to justify his popularity with me, there was always the superior eating quality of his firm, white flesh. To me, Pickerel are right up there with the best of all fishes when it comes to flavor. I think the only reason he is not at, or near, the top of everyone's list is because of the numerous, fine, "y" shaped bones located in the thickest portions of his flesh.

This was no problem for me, because I learned where they were located and watched for them and removed them as I ate. You have to pay a price

57

for all things worthwhile. It's just as well the Pickerel is constructed in this manner, because if he weren't, he would probably be extinct because he is so easy to catch.

The fish of which I speak is technically called the Eastern Chain Pickerel; not the Walleyed Pike of the Mid-west. Its Latin name is *Esox Niger*; the Black Pike. Although most people might think of him as ugly, possibly because of the many rows of very sharp pointed teeth in a mouth sometimes appearing to be longer than his body, he is in reality, a rather beautiful fish. He possesses a body that is perfectly designed for the niche that he fills in Mother Nature's grand scheme of things. His body is long, slender, and streamlined. He has a flattened and pointed snout that enables him to shoot through the water at an astonishing rate of speed for short distances. His head makes up a good quarter or more of his total body length and of that head; about half is tooth-studded mouth. He is the Barracuda of freshwater ponds and lakes.

His soft dorsal and anal fins are set far back on his body, adding to his streamlined appearance and probably assisting him with his incredible acceleration when scared or in pursuit of prey. His coloration is distinctive. He has a dark green or nearly black back, accounting for his Latin name. His sides are of a greenish, bronze coloration, covered with connecting chain markings rather like hexagonal chicken wire that has been stretched out lengthways. This gives reason for his common name of Eastern Chain Pickerel. His belly is usually white or cream colored.

It is possible to confuse him with the Northern Pike where their ranges overlap. A good way to positively distinguish between the two if uncertainty arises is to compare their cheeks and gill covers. (pre-opercula and opercula to those among us who must be totally correct.) The Pickerel has scales completely covering both cheek and gill cover while a Northern Pike's gill covers (opercula) have scales only on the upper half.

His appetite; which is legendary, is his eventual downfall. It's recorded that he will eat just about anything in his domain that he can slide down his gullet, including insects when he is young and other fish; even his own species, when mature. He has been known to include young muskrats or even ducklings in his diet, when available.

In recent years, I caught a Pickerel in Lower Sabao Lake in Hancock County, Maine. He wasn't particularly large; about sixteen inches long, and had a peculiar bulge in his belly. Feeling along the bulge with my fingers, I could feel the four legs, head and the hard shell of a small turtle. The turtle was about two and a half inches in diameter. I shook my head in amazement because the turtle was actually wider than the Pickerel's head! To top that off, I had caught the fish on a Dardevil spoon that was three inches long. I don't know where that fish thought he was going to put the lure. I released the ambitious fish with the thought that he would probably eat himself to death in the near future.

My favorite method for catching a Pickerel was by using a dead shiner. This provided me with double pleasure because, first, I had to catch the shiner and then use the shiner to catch the Pickerel. Catching shiners can be a challenge, also. Shiners have soft, tiny mouths and are not the easiest fish in the word to catch. Getting them to bite was not the problem; *hooking* them was. You can catch one occasionally with a size six hook, but that is just luck. The method that my brother and I finally settled on was to use a tiny hook of about size ten or twelve baited with an equally tiny piece of garden worm, (not a night crawler) just enough to cover the point of the hook. When the shiner bit, we let it run with the bait it until we could see the bait disappear. That meant that the bait was either in the shiner's mouth or that the shiner was headed directly away from you. Both were good signs.

That was when you set the hook, and if luck was with you, a shiner was flipped aboard the raft. It was quickly dispatched with a pinch of the fingers behind its head and laid on the floor of the raft to await the arrival of some more of its companions.

When enough bait was caught, we poled the raft to within easy casting distance of some lily pads and anchored it. The easiest way was to push the pole through a hole in the raft's floor and then into the soft bottom of the Cove. One of the recently deceased shiners was then selected and impaled on a larger size, long shanked hook such as a number four or six Carlisle. We usually inserted the point of the hook into the mouth of the shiner and then brought it out through the top of its head just behind its eyes. This gives the dead shiner a very natural look on the retrieve.

Hooked up in this manner, the bait was cast just beyond a group of lily pads and was allowed to sink a few inches into the water before the retrieve was begun. The retrieve was made with a series of soft, quick little snaps of the rod tip. This caused the minnow to scoot through the water in an erratic manner that was calculated to drive any Pickerel that saw it, wild with lust.

After each little snap of the rod tip was made, the bait was allowed to settle for a few seconds before the next snap. Usually, during one of these slight pauses was the time when a Pickerel would attack. Bait fished in this manner seems to be irresistible to a Pickerel, even if he has dined only moments before.

We lost a lot of pickerel in the beginning until we learned how a Pickerel behaves after he has taken the bait. If you strike immediately after the bait is taken, it is almost a certainty you will not get the fish. In fact, he probably will not even feel the hook and you will have served him up a free meal, for which he will not even thank you.

A Pickerel almost always catches a minnow from the side, leaving its head and tail protruding from both sides of its mouth. That explains why bait hooked up in this manner will cause you to lose a fish if you try to set the hook as soon as the Pickerel strikes. After the Pickerel takes the bait, he usually makes a short run to deeper water and then comes to a stop. After a moment or so, if you watch your line closely where it enters the water, you can tell when he starts to work the bait around, with a series of little chomps, into a position to be swallowed head first. After the bait is swallowed, he will usually swim off again to his old haunts in the lily pads or to some other favorite spot. This is when you set the hook . . . hard! Remember, the hook is in a large piece of bait and if you strike easily, the hook may not set properly. If you set it hard, the chances are now very good that you have your fish firmly impaled.

Hooking a good size Pickerel and landing him, are two different things. When a Pickerel feels the hook, he has but one thing in mind . . . *head for cover!* And head for cover he does! A quick, powerful lunge into the nearest weed bed or patch of lily pads is his favorite tactic. This can cause the line to become entangled to the point that it will break or he can tear himself free if he is not firmly hooked. A Pickerel's best friend when hooked is a patch of thick weeds.

If you succeed in keeping him from the weeds or lily pads and in open water, he still has a trick or two up his scaly sleeves. A twenty-inch Pickerel of two pounds or more can put up a fight that will gain the respect of even the most skeptical of fishermen. He can dive and make many short but powerful runs. Although not famed for his leaping abilities, as is the Atlantic Salmon or the Small Mouth Bass, Mr. Pickerel can and will leap if the opportunity arises.

If you have caught the fish on a spoon and ease up the pressure on the line at any time while he is near the surface, such as when he is near the boat while you are trying to land him, he may give a Tarpon-like leap complete with a rattling of gill covers and a shaking of his head that might surprise you. A word of warning . . . you may have to duck a spoon with treble hooks as it dislodges and flies back at you.

If you follow the procedures that I have described when using live, dead, or cut bait, I guarantee that your success rate will increase when fishing for Pickerel. One other piece of important information is this; use a fine wire leader when fishing for them. Their sharp teeth can slice through a piece of braided line of most any weight like it wasn't there. A monofilament line is a little tougher for them to slice through, but if a battle is of any length at all, the Pickerel is sure to win.

Trevor and I have discovered that one of the best baits of all for Pickerel is a four or five inch strip cut from one of their own white bellies. This is fished in the same manner as a dead shiner. This bait is very soft and pliable and ripples as it is pulled through the water. The skin is incredibly tough and it is possible to use one piece to catch several Pickerel. Be sure to check your game laws to see if this is legal in your area. I have probably made it sound as if pickerel eat all the time. This is not really the case at all. There were times when the pickerel seemed to have sore mouths and would eat only enough to survive. Other times, when the water temperatures became too warm, they got lethargic and would rather just find the shade of a good lily patch and not move. At my age, I know how they feel.

On some of these sunny, windless days, even if we had no bait or lures, we could still bring a few fish home for supper with no bait at all. We would pole the raft slowly and quietly through the beds of lily pads; our eyes peeled for fish. The Pickerel were usually hovering under the lily pads with snouts pointed out, waiting for dinner to swim by. They were easily spotted if you knew their habits and knew where to look.

When one was spotted, one of us would cast an un-baited hook over and beyond the Pickerel and drag the line toward the fish until it was draped over his back. Then, with a quick yank and a little luck, the fish was hooked and the fight was on. With no luck, all you would have was a scale on the point of the hook and the familiar boiling of water where he used to be.

A foul hooked Pickerel seems to pull even harder than one that is hooked in the mouth. It is almost as if you put a harness on him and yelled, "Mush!" No acrobatics or fooling around this time, only a fish pulling as hard as he can in one direction and you pulling as hard as you can in the other. That is the way it is until he either breaks loose or you manage to land him. This is probably illegal, also, so consider this to be a method to be used only if you are lost in the wilds of Canada with no bait on hand and you are dying of starvation. Maybe you will be forgiven for breaking a law to save your own life. Please note that I said, "Maybe."

This is probably more than you either knew or wanted to know about Pickerel fishing . . . but there you have it anyway. However, I think you may find that after a slow day of salmon or trout fishing, trying your luck on a good Pickerel pond might add some pleasure to your life as it did to my brother's and mine.

CHAPTER NINE

The Worlds Biggest Sucker

EACH SPRING IN April or early May, Johnson Brook is the scene of one of Mother Nature's minor spectaculars. This is when the suckers start their annual spawning run. They come by the hundreds, traveling upstream, mostly in the late evening hours and at night, to spawn in the shallow, rocky-bottomed areas of the brook. After spawning, they gradually drop back down stream, holing up in the deeper pools by day.

If a beauty contest were held in the State of Maine for fresh water fish, undoubtedly the Brook Trout would be crowned king or queen. On the other hand, the poor sucker would be hard pressed to keep from finishing dead last; but possibly ahead of the Hornpout. Round fleshy mouths attached to the bottom of blunt, square heads growing on broad shouldered bodies are three solid strikes against the sucker when it comes to beauty.

Most Mainers would put this fish at the bottom of the list of piscatorial pleasure when it comes to dining, also. Although it's true the Sucker does not compare to the Brook Trout or Atlantic Salmon in flavor, its bony flesh is sweet enough in the early spring when the waters are still clear and icy cold. The same criticisms can be made of other fish, even the trout and salmon, when taken from warm, muddy waters.

The male suckers seem to out number the females. This is possibly because of the way that I have seen them mating. It seems that two males might be required to fertilize the female's eggs during spawning. I have observed this many times by flashlight at night on the spawning beds. A female is trapped between two males and the males press the female between them. With much quivering and shaking, the eggs of the female are deposited on the rocky streambed and are fertilized by milt from the males. At this time, the males have a band of red color down each side. I don't know what the significance of these red bands may be, but I'm sure the lady suckers must know.

After spawning, the sucker proves she is as good a mother as she is beautiful. She abandons the eggs and leaves them on their own. We can't hold this against her, of course, because the beautiful Brook Trout and Atlantic Salmon also make orphans of their young.

I was always glad when the suckers returned. It was a sure sign that spring had come at last and it was also a sure cure for the most dreaded of all north woods illnesses, cabin fever. The annual sucker run provided an interlude of fun and sport when it was most needed. They came when it was too late for ice fishing, but still too early to pursue the Brook Trout with any degree of success.

The old timers have always said, "Trout won't bite until the leaves on the trees are as big as a mouse's ear." I can't vouch for the truth of that argument, but I have noticed that at about the same time the leaves reach mouse ear proportions, aquatic insects are hatching and the water has warmed up slightly. So who is to say what causes the trout to start biting at this time. Regardless of the reasons, mouse-eared leaves can still be regarded as a fairly reliable indicator of when to break out your trout gear in Maine.

Although suckers can be caught on a baited hook, the most effective method on shallow brooks and streams is to use a fish spear. This type of fishing is done at night by wading in the shallows while the fish are on, or traveling to, the spawning beds. You locate the fish by use of a lantern or flashlight.

A fish spear usually has from three to five barbed tines that are three or four inches long and are attached to a shaft of about five or six feet in length. We could never afford to buy one, so Yankee ingenuity again had to be brought into play. My spear was much cheaper and simpler than a store-bought spear. I made mine from an old broom or mop handle. I started by wrapping a layer of fine wire around the end that was to receive the "tine", if you will. This fine wire, hopefully, would prevent the end of my new spear shaft from splitting when the long nail that I would use as my spear point was driven into the end of the shaft. I then filed the head of the nail to a sharp point, and presto! I had a one tined, but barbless, fish spear!

Having no barb on the tine to prevent a fish from sliding off, meant that my spearing technique had to be modified slightly. With a conventional barbed fish spear, you spot the fish with the light held in one hand and the spear in the other. You kept the fish in the beam of light and, sneaking up on it from downstream, you speared it with the other hand and walked ashore with your catch. This is a fairly simple operation.

With only one tine and no barb, the technique required was to spear the fish with one hand and hold it to the bottom with the spear. Then you had to reach down into the water with the other hand and grab the fish so that it would not slide off the barbless tine and escape. It becomes obvious after spearing the fish you have a problem. What do you do with the light?

I eventually solved this problem by just sticking the flashlight into a pocket and feeling my way to shore in the dark with my feet. When you are young, however, you don't always think of the obvious. Most of the time you don't think at all until the problem is upon you.

The first fish I speared successfully; I say successfully because there were many misses and near misses that showed up the shortcomings of a one-tined, barbless spear, the fish nearly escaped each time that I tried to lift it from the water. I solved the flashlight problem by simply sticking the end of the flashlight into my mouth.

Have you ever tried to walk through a fast current in a rocky-bottomed brook at night with a wriggling, fish in one hand still attached to the spear, and a two-celled flashlight stuck in your mouth? It's not easy to point a flashlight that is in a death grip between your teeth no matter how strong your jaws are. The light flopped around in my mouth; first in one direction and then in another. By the time I got to shore, my jaws felt as if I would never be able to chew again, my teeth ached and I had drooled about a quart and a half. That is to not mention all the gagging that I had done!

Being a fast learner, on the next attempt I stuck the flashlight under my right arm. It was much easier to walk ashore that way and much easier still on the teeth, but it was still awkward to hold a struggling fish down with an arm that had a flashlight growing from its armpit. I gave up on that technique after dropping the flashlight into the brook. I had to walk back home through the dark woods with no light that night. Fortunately for me, there was a nearly full moon that gave some light for me to see by.

Most of the suckers in the brook would be between twelve and eighteen inches long. Occasionally you might get one that was over twenty inches long that could weigh as much as three pounds. I mention this because after you have fished for a while, the size of a fish takes on some importance to a fisherman. I have never yet met a fisherman who, in the deep, dark recesses of his mind, didn't dream of catching the largest fish recorded of his favorite species, whether it be sucker or salmon. One fateful night it seemed to me that I had been selected to become the boy who had speared the largest sucker in the world. What follows, is how that opportunity came about.

After a few years of experience, I became somewhat worldly and selective about my sucker spearing. It had become an easy thing now, and not much of a challenge. So now, Bud Simpson the great spearer of suckers selected only the biggest and best specimens for his spear. No more indiscriminate spearing for me!

It had become so easy that I developed what I called the Simpson Method of Sucker Removal, SMSR for short. Again, one of the sporting magazines had steered me onto this new method. I had read an article describing a method called, "tickling catfish". It told of a technique used down south where one of the locals would feel very gently under the banks of the river with his hands until he located a catfish. He would then caress or "tickle" the fish until he was able to stick his hand into the gill covers or mouth of the fish and toss it ashore. I had laughed at the time and wondered what would have happened if he had accidentally "tickled" an alligator. I had taken that story with a grain of salt, but later in life I found out that this was indeed a way to catch those fish.

I thought of that article one night (most of my greatest thoughts seem to come to me at night) as I was selectively pursuing the sucker population of Johnson Brook. I decided to give "tickling" a try. The first fish that I tried it on splashed water in my face and was gone. *Not gentle enough*, I thought. I tried it again several more times until at last I must have developed just the right touch and was actually able to get a grip on one before it twisted away. Then another great thought came to me. Maybe, I thought, if I tried it on only female suckers it would work better. After all, didn't they hang around when the males nuzzled them? Besides, the females were usually bigger than the males, anyway.

This seemed to work out better so I kept at it until I finally perfected the SMSR method. I found that the best way was to select one from a group. They seemed less wary than single specimens. Walking upstream, I would come up behind the fish as quietly as I could. I would gently put my hand in the water a few feet behind the fish and very slowly move it through the water until it was over the fish's back and just behind its head. I could then reach down and with my finger tips, lightly touch its back until my fingers were in a position just behind its gills. Then, with a quick squeeze, I could then lift the sucker from the water without a single flop or wriggle. Gripping the fish at this spot seemed to paralyze it.

I don't know if this method would work at any other time of the year or only at spawning time. The secret seemed to be patience with no sudden moves and a minimum of disturbance in the water. I eventually got good enough at this to be able to gently move the suckers around in the water without alarming them to the point where they would swim away.

One night while amusing myself using the SMSR on the unsuspecting suckers, I heard a commotion in the water behind me. It sounded as if a whole school of suckers was trying to swim over a shallow spot behind me. I turned and pointed my light at the spot of the disturbance. It was not a *school* of fish; it was only *one* fish! Its body was only half covered by the water at that spot and it was wriggling furiously; water splashing everywhere, trying to get into the deeper water of the pool I was standing in. It was hard for me to believe there was a sucker as big as that one in the whole world.

With a final thrust of its tail, it glided into the pool and swam past me. My eyes must have looked as if they were going to fall out. The fish swam to the head of the pool and settled in behind a large boulder in some waist deep water, its body slowly undulating as it held itself in position.

I assessed the situation as quickly as I could. The water the big fish was in was deeper than I would have liked. If I bent over and tried to take him with my hands, my face might be under water. I decided to use my trusty spear. I slowly walked upstream and the closer I came to the fish, the deeper the cold waters became until they had crept up my body nearly to my waist. The water was much deeper than I had at first thought. I looked down at the fish as he slowly fanned his fins in the eddy behind the rock. He seemed to be bigger than ever. More than three feet long, I thought! This had to be the biggest one ever; maybe the biggest one in the world!

I put the spear into the water and moved it into position behind the fish's head. This was going to be easy! The fish didn't move except for its tail and fins and the slight undulation of its body. Then I thrust the spear forward. The spear struck home and it seemed for a moment that I had stabbed a stick of dynamite! The water literally exploded and the shaft of the spear cracked me across the face as something big, cold and wet hit me in the chest. In the next instant, I found myself sitting in chin deep water with one hand holding the flashlight over my head and the other bracing the spear on the bottom to keep me from going completely under. Between my frantic gasps for breath from the shock of the icy immersion, I could hear the great fish splashing through the water, heading upstream for parts unknown. I struggled erect and headed for shore. I had not expected such a violent reaction and was more than a little shook up.

The point on my spear was bent at an extreme angle. I could hardly believe what had happened. Shivering and chilled to the bone, I headed for the warmth of my home and a set of dry clothes.

The next day I walked to my grandfather's house and told him of my experience of the night before. When I mentioned the size of the fish, I noticed his eyebrows rise a little and a twinkle came to his eyes. I thought for a moment that he did not believe me.

"Did this big sucker have any spots on it?" he asked.

I concentrated on the image of that fish in my mind for a moment. Then it dawned on me that maybe that fish had not been a sucker at all. "Yes, it did," I replied. "How did you know?"

My grandfather slapped his leg with his open palm and laughed gleefully. "That, young fella, was no sucker. That was a *salmon!*"

He laughed again and bellowed, "You're gonna need somethin' a little more rugged than a matchstick with a pin in it if you're gonna tangle with one o' them!"

As you know, that was not the first time that I had been up close and personal with a salmon without realizing what it was. This time I had engaged one in personal hand to hand combat. It had been a very impressive first hand meeting. Now that I knew what these fish looked like, I was hoping for *another* meeting sometime in the near future.

CHAPTER TEN

I *Finally* Win One with Salmo Salar

DURING THE LATE Forties and throughout the Fifties, State of Maine wildlife officials had pretty much written off the Atlantic Salmon in the Penobscot River. According to them and some of the local sports writers, the river was too polluted to support a viable population of this species. My brother and I agreed with them to a point; not that they had ever asked us. We knew first-hand that the salmon were making a valiant effort on their own to survive in their ancestral waters of the Penobscot River. We would find many dead bodies of these salmon floating in the polluted waters of the river proper. We had, however, also seen them at the entrance to many of the cooler, comparatively unpolluted brooks and streams flowing into the Penobscot between the Veazie and Bangor dams and even below the Bangor dam. I believe firmly that a small, tough population of these great fish managed to hold onto life on their own during those trying years.

If the fishway had been maintained properly during these years, their comeback in later years would have been much easier and less expensive than it became. Even though it was denied, we saw first hand that the fishway was closed at the Bangor dam. It seemed to be closed most frequently during open season on Atlantic Salmon. We wondered if this might have something to do with keeping salmon in the pools below the dam for the pleasure of salmon fishermen.

I vividly remember one day in particular. My brother and I had gone down to the Bangor dam for one reason or another. We decided to see if we could see any fish in the fishway. What we saw amazed us! The entire length of the fishway was clogged with the bodies of tens of thousands of dead alewives. We couldn't believe our eyes. They were blocked from going any further upstream because the fishway was closed off. A few days later, we went back to look into the fishway again and an even more amazing sight greeted our eyes. You literally could not see the alewives anymore. Their rotting carcasses were covered with more maggots than you would ever see in your worst nightmare! It appeared as if the bodies of the poor fish were actually moving because of the unbelievable number of maggots covering them.

As I said before, the fish and game people denied ever closing the fishway except for maintenance purposes. All I can say to that is this: I would not want to have been the people who had to clean up that particular mess. Maybe they just opened the gate and flushed it all downstream like a gigantic toilet.

As we poled our rafts around the Cove in different years, we had the opportunity to see many large salmon swimming around in the shallows of The Cove. They swam in large circles from the deeper waters to the shallows and back again, almost as if they were searching for something. I'm certain also, that years ago, the headwaters of Johnson Brook had been a spawning ground for salmon. In the mid-Fifties, I had seen salmon in the brook, and had also found a dead one, as far upstream as Eastern Avenue in Brewer. My grandfather once told me of a large twenty pound salmon he had shot before World War II. He had been deer hunting near the brook when he spotted it in a pool below the power line. He didn't get his deer that day but had brought home the big salmon instead.

One hot summer day, I was casting a Johnson Silver Minnow spoon from the raft toward the entrance of the brook near the sandbar. I had seen some movement of the waters there and it looked as if a large fish was swimming around. The first thing that popped into my mind was that it might be one of the large bass that usually stay in the deeper waters, but had swum into the shallows. This happened occasionally but not too often. I made several casts ahead of the movement with no luck, so I poled the raft in a little closer to see if I could see what was making this disturbance in the water.

The waters of the Cove were not crystal clear, especially in the warm months of summer. They were usually clear enough, though, to identify fish if they were not too deep in the water. Even closer in, I could not see the fish clearly because it had disturbed the silt on the bottom of the shallows. As I watched closely, I realized that there was more than one fish making bow waves in the water, and if they were bass, they had to have been world record fish.

I knew enough now at this point in my life; with a little more salmon experience behind me, to realize that, possibly, these fish were salmon. I also knew, according to the more renowned sports writers of the day, Atlantic Salmon never ate during their stay in fresh water and they would *never* hit a spoon. Specifically, they would never hit a spoon the size of my silver minnow, which was about three inches or more in length. But, hope springs eternal in the breast of a young and ignorant fisherman, so I continued to cast to these fish.

Every time they made their pass through the area, I cast; time and time again. I had just about given up on the idea of catching one of them when something heavy bumped the lure. It didn't feel like a bite, just a heavy drag on the line. I thought one of these fish had only brushed against the line, but I pulled the rod tip back half-heartedly anyway, and the water exploded as a salmon leaped high into the air only fifteen or so feet from the raft. It seemed as if it were happening in slow motion. Too late I decided to set the hook properly, and when I did, the heavy yank pulled the lure out of his mouth and it came zooming back over my shoulder just missing my ear by inches.

The salmon seemed to fall slowly back into the water, landing on its side and making a bigger splash than it had when it had leaped so high into my vision. I yelled at the top of my lungs, "Oh noooo!" as if that would put him back on my line and give me another chance. I got on my knees and pounded my fists on the floor of the raft, vowing to never again set a hook so weakly on a fish as large as that salmon.

There were very few days during the spring, summer and fall months that Trevor or I, or both of us together, were not at the Cove or on the brook. It was almost certain that one of us would run into a salmon again. As usual, things like this happen when you least expect it. I was, however, *mentally* prepared for this moment when and wherever it might be.

One late summer afternoon, my brother and I had walked to the Cove and were standing in the pine grove across from the mouth of the brook. We looked across the Cove and saw a friend of ours, Rodney Dunton, fishing in the brook. We called across to him to find out what he was fishing for.

"There are some really big bass over here and I'm trying to catch one," he yelled back.

Trevor and I looked at each other and apparently had the same thought. Large bass did *not* hang out at the spot he was fishing. The water was too shallow and there was no shelter for them. That is not to say that it was impossible, just very unlikely. We were curious about the situation and decided to go over to the brook's mouth and see what Rodney was trying to catch. I thought that it might possibly be some large Pickerel even though I knew that they did not usually swim around. They lay in wait.

We climbed down the bank of the pine grove and walked to our left. We got to where Rodney was by following along the shore of the Little Cove to the mouth of the brook. When we were nearly there, we could see him casting something out into the water among the rocks. The bait or lure made quite a splash as it landed in the water.

"What are you using for bait?" we called.

"I have a frog," he replied.

Finally we arrived at the spot where he was fishing. Indeed, he *did* have a frog! It was the biggest frog that I had seen in quite a while and looked as though it might weigh in at a half-pound or more. Well, I thought to myself, if there is a bass or pickerel here, it had probably departed and was all the way out into the river when that poor frog smacked into the water.

Much to our amazement, the fish that he was fishing for was still there. And again, much to our amazement, we saw there was more than one of them. They were swimming among the rocks in the shallow water in that now familiar circle.

My heart skipped a beat as I took a closer look at one of them as it swam by Rodney. Sure enough, they were salmon! Trevor realized what they were at about the same time as I.

"You're not going to catch *them* with a frog, Rodney," he said excitedly. "Those are *salmon!*"

Both of our hearts were racing now. Here was our chance to catch one of those big fish that had treated me so miserably in the past! I may have been prepared mentally for this task, but tackle-wise I was totally unprepared. All I had were a few hooks and a spinner or two and some worms that we had intended to catch some baitfish with. The spinner had a feathered treble hook on it though, and that spawned an idea in my head.

"Maybe we can hook one if we take the spinner off this thing and just use the triple hook," I suggested.

By "hooking one", I did not mean casting it out and hoping one might take it in a conventional manner. I meant to use it to jig or snag one in its body as it swam by. The legality of this type of fishing did not enter our minds at our tender ages. There were salmon swimming by and our only thought was how to get one before they disappeared. Impatiently, we waited until the big moment arrived and one of the salmon started to head in our direction again.

As he swam by, I attempted to cast the triple hook over his back and I give it a yank but the fish had already swum by before the hook could sink down to the depth where he was in the water. The feathers on the hook caused it to sink at a much slower rate than a bare hook. In order to snag one, the timing of the cast would have to be nearly perfect. I tried once or twice more with no success.

Finally I came up with a new plan. I would cast the hook out into the water and let it settle to the bottom. Then, when the salmon swam over it, I would give the line a sharp upward pull and maybe the hook would find a home somewhere in the salmon's body.

I cast the line out according to the new master plan, let it settle to the bottom across the path of the circling fish and then waited. A moment or two later, along came Mr. Salmon headed for exactly the right spot! As he swam over the line, I felt it move as the big fish brushed against it. I gave the line a hard yank and sure enough, the hook sank home. The salmon did not slow down a bit. In fact, He seemed to know he was in trouble and headed downstream, by the flat rock, out through the channel by the point and seemed to be headed for the Atlantic Ocean. I had never felt a fish pull so hard. Even the biggest Pickerel I had ever caught using this method never pulled as hard as this fish did. It was as though a Bangor & Aroostook steam engine had attached itself to the line and was heading for parts unknown!

I wondered if I had enough line on my reel to hold him. I had hooked him somewhere near the tail and that turned out to be fortunate. I found out later in my poaching career that the closer they are hooked to the shoulder, the harder and longer they can fight. They seem to lose energy faster if the tail is forced to work harder, as when there is pressure on it from a hook and line.

Finally, just as the line was nearly exhausted from the reel, he slowed down and the tide was turned. I began to regain more and more line between runs and finally I dragged him back into the shallows. I slowly pulled him to the waters near my feet. Trevor lifted the exhausted fish from the water with both hands and tossed him up onto the bank and we all scrambled up to inspect it. It was not huge by some standards but it was by far the largest fish I had ever caught.

A fresh run Atlantic Salmon is a beautiful fish. This one looked as if it had been in the river for a while, but it was still relatively bright and silvery with a dark back. A few spots showed on its sides, but there were not as many as I had expected. From my encounter with the one I had speared in the brook, I had a mental picture of a fish with many spots on it.

Trevor and Rodney and I had never seen a fish this large lying at our feet before. It probably weighed in at about eight or nine pounds but he had felt much heavier when he was at the end of my line. Before this moment, I did not really think I was ever going to catch one of these big fish. The Atlantic Salmon had been only an image in my head put there by disbelieving eyes and fed by high hopes. But, there he was, the fulfillment of a young angler's dream. *Salmo Salar*, the mighty Atlantic Salmon had finally lost a battle to the Simpson boys.

CHAPTER ELEVEN

Bud's Pets; Ya Gotta Love 'em

WHEN YOU ARE young and spend many of the waking hours of your time in the great outdoors, you quite naturally meet up with many different species of wildlife in your wanderings. I was no different than any kid in the same situation and would occasionally bring home one of my wild friends. Whenever I brought one home with me, the inevitable answer to my query, "Can I keep it?" was the equally inevitable answer, "Your father will have a fit if he sees you with that thing."

Trevor almost had a wild pet once. He was returning to the house along the path from the direction of the river. I met him near the wild apple tree by the path. "Guess what," he stated, "I just killed a red squirrel with a rock." I guess it must be genetic. We Simpsons seem to have a knack for rock throwing.

Apparently he had seen a red squirrel in one of the trees and threw a rock at it and had knocked it out of the tree. "Where is it?" I asked.

"I've got it in my pocket," he said as he put his hand into the pocket of his jeans. Suddenly he yelled in pain and out of the pocket came the hand with the squirrel firmly attached to one of his fingers! Fortunately, the squirrel released his bite on the finger and scrambled away and up the nearest tree. I'm sure though, if the squirrel had been just a little groggier instead of angry, we would have tried to make a pet of him.

The first specimen of wildlife I can recall bringing home was an absolutely beautiful emerald green snake. He had a deep yellow, almost orange belly, and was about a foot long. I just loved the way he kept sticking out his tongue at everyone. I didn't know that this was the way a snake "smelled" his surroundings; "tasting" the air, so to speak. This aided him in finding food. The result of my question of whether I could keep him or not was a loud shriek from my mother followed by an even louder, "Get that thing out of here!"

I left the house quickly but this time I did not let the snake go. I found a small cardboard box and put my friend in it. I threw in a few handfuls of fresh grass and a cricket for food and put the box out on the back porch. I checked him every day and threw in grasshoppers and more crickets for his dining pleasure. Then one day I heard my father say, "What in the hell is in this box?" Needless to say, the snake was history.

One morning I had walked down to the river by way of Mr. Dean's path with the intention of walking to the Cove. I must not have been to the Cove for several days because when I got to the sandy shore, I saw something unusual at the edge of the water that I could not have missed. It was a wooden box about eighteen inches square and it had been sunk into the sand close to the water's edge so that only a couple of inches showed above the sand. I walked over to the box and looked in. The bottom of the box was a foot or so below the water line of the river and water had filled it to within six inches of the top.

There, floating on the surface of the water within the box, were two young muskrats. One of them had drowned and the survivor was using the dead one as a sort of life raft. He was very weak and barely able to stay afloat. I ran home as quickly as I could and brought back a cardboard box. I carefully bent over the box and touched the little muskrat. He offered no resistance, so I lifted him out of the water and put him into the cardboard box.

Off I went; back up the path with my new found friend. Strangely enough, my mother did not put up too much of a fuss after I had told her how I had found him. Encouraged, I dried him off with a dry piece of cloth and wrapped him in an old tee shirt. After he had dried off and his fur had fluffed up a little, he looked downright cute. He was just a little round ball of fluff with beady little black eyes on one end and a straight, skinny little tail sticking out the other. He seemed to appreciate my rescuing him and settled down for a much deserved rest and a nap. I put a couple of boards across the top of the box so he couldn't get out until I had a chance to build a cage for him.

A few hours later I decided to look in on him to see how he was doing. I carefully moved one of the boards off so I could catch a look at him. He was lying there asleep, so I took the other board off and reached in to pet him. The moment that my hand touched him, it was as if this cute, fuzzy little creature had transformed into the rat from hell! He bared his long, yellow teeth at me and squealed and hissed while trying to bite my hand. Those cute, beady little eyes had become evil and looked as if they belonged to the devil himself!

As quickly as I could, I slammed one board back onto the top of the box and then the other. Fortunately for me, he decided that hunkering down in the back of the box was his best defense instead of a charge at his perceived new enemy; me.

Chagrined, I carried the box with its furious occupant back down to the river and released him. He ran from the box and headed straight out into the river as if he did not intend to stop until he reached the other side. I pulled up the wooden box so he would not get trapped in it again. I later found out this was a way of trapping muskrats by some of the Indians who ran trap lines along the Penobscot River. They would set a wooden box into a sandy shore and bait it with parsnips. Apparently, muskrats love parsnips and would jump into the water filled box for a lunch and then they could not climb back up its steep sides.

Our house, being as open as it was to the elements, was no barrier to the smaller wildlife in the area. By smaller wildlife, I mean mice in particular and sometimes a rat or two. One day while lying on my bed in my upstairs bedroom reading, I saw a cute little field mouse run across the floor. Being in urgent need of a pet, a thought entered my always active mind. *Wouldn't it be nice if you had a mouse for a pet?* But how could I get one. Money was no barrier here. After all, mice were free.

There is an absolutely amazing wealth of information available to inquiring young minds written in sporting magazines. As luck would have it; the week before spotting this mouse, I had read an article describing how to build a box trap. All I would have to do was to scale the plans down to mouse proportions. I set about the task and before the day was over, I had what I felt was a serviceable trap I made from a wooden cheese box. It measured about four by four by six inches.

The front of the trap was a door with a cloth hinge glued to one end and to the top of the box. I tied a string to a small nail driven into the bottom of the door. I passed it up and over the top of the box and ran it back into the box through a hole I had punched with a nail through the back of the box. I tied a piece of cracker to the end of the string, which was just long enough to hold the door up to about forty-five degrees from the horizontal. According to the Simpson theory of mouse trapping, when the mouse ate the cracker crumb, the string would slip back out through the hole and the door then slams shut and captures said mouse. The door was held closed with a small piece of flat, thin metal that was bent back upon itself and formed a crude hook.

I set the trap before going to bed that night and when I woke up the next morning, I saw the door of the trap was shut! Even more amazing than that, I could hear a sound inside telling me there might indeed be a mouse in it. After breakfast, I built a cage of sorts for my soon to be pet mouse. It was just an old wooden box that I had nailed a tattered piece of metal window screen to the open side. I had cut a small square hole into what was now the top. A piece of board with a rock on top of it would keep the mouse from escaping.

I picked up the box trap and took it to the cage. I quickly opened the door to the trap and in the same motion, dumped its contents through the hole in the top of the cage. My eyes opened wide with wonder! There were *two* mice in the trap! It had worked much better than I had hoped. The trap worked so well that in a week or two, I had more mouse pets than I could use.

I noticed that three of the mice had small white blazes on their foreheads. These little white spots set them apart from the rest of the herd. I decided I had too many mice on hand, so I took my cage out back and released all but the ones with the mark on their heads. I decided the only ones I would keep from now on were the unusual ones. I trapped more mice over the following weeks, keeping only the ones with the mark and releasing all the others out back of the house in the woods. Pretty soon it seemed that I had more of the marked ones than I could handle.

Then it happened. My mother found my mouse stash and issued an ultimatum. I tried to convince her that even though I had a couple of dozen mice in the cage, I had caught many more than that and then let them go outside the house so that really meant that there were *less* mice in the house than before. My logical argument fell on deaf ears and off to the woods went my two dozen pet mice. I didn't realize it at that time, but women see mice in a different light than young boys.

My grandfather kept two skunks as pets in a large cage in his barn at Eddington Bend where routes 9 and 178 intersect. His house overlooked the Penobscot River with a good view all the way up to the Veazie dam and down the river towards The Cove. For two years in a row, the pair of skunks delivered him a litter of little ones on Mother's Day. He had the young skunks de-scented and gave them away to any one who might want an unusual pet. Skunks make very tame and lovable pets if they are treated kindly.

I happily accepted his offer to adopt one of the little offspring. I brought it home and it quickly declared our house to be his, also. This must have happened at a time when my father was not living in the house because I don't remember any objections to my skunk from that direction. Being an original thinker, I christened him "Stinky", not for his odor but for his heritage. He slept in a closet area in the front room and built a cozy nest for himself by hauling anything made of paper into his area and tearing it up. He would roam about the house at night and if any paper was within reach, it ended up in his ever-growing nest.

He seemed to enjoy his role as Simpson house skunk. When he was up and about during the day, he would walk or run around the outer perimeter of the front room. He did this for what seemed like hours at a time. He ate anything that was available. Thank God for omnivorous animals. If you teased him, he would first stamp his front feet on the floor and sway back and forth. If you really got him aggravated, he would stand up on his front feet and turn his backside towards you in an agitated manner and if his gun had been loaded, I'm sure that he would have let you have a shot right between your eyes. We gave him back to my grandfather after a while, probably for the same reasons that caused us to get rid of all our other pets.

One day a car stopped in front of our house and the woman who was driving it asked me what kind of a bird was in the pasture across from our house. I looked across the road and a large seagull was sitting on a rock in the pasture. It was not too unusual to see seagulls in this area because of the river down back and we were only about forty or fifty miles from the ocean. I told her what it was and she was on her way.

A couple of hours went by and when I looked again, the seagull was still there on the same rock. That did seem to be a little unusual, so I decided to have a closer look. I climbed the fence and walked toward the gull. I got closer and closer and it didn't fly away. Then I saw why. His left eye was injured and he could not see me as I approached him from that side. When I got to him, he saw me but for some reason did not get excited or try to fly away. I picked him up and carried him back across the street to the house.

I was met with the usual, "get that damn thing out of here" argument from my father, so I carried the bird down to the river and set him down on the shore. I felt a little sad as I walked away, because the bird tuned around and started to walk towards me. I ran up the path towards the house for a few yards to get out of its sight. I walked the rest of the way and went about the business of being a boy, throwing rocks, climbing trees and the usual things a boy does to delay having to do any chores.

I finally got home and sat on the back porch. A movement along the path that I had taken from the river caught my eye. I looked and there, walking up the path towards the house, was the one-eyed seagull. I briefly thought of using the old argument of, "It followed me home, Mama, can I keep it?" I knew by now this argument would never work, so I kept him on the back porch for the night and released him on the island in The Cove the next day. I don't think he held that against me because he finally flew away in strange half-circles in the general direction of the Atlantic Ocean.

The last wild pet of any note we had was a crow. I was an adult at this time approaching the time when I was to get my draft notice for the military. My brother and I were fishing where Diamond Rock is located just below The Cove. We heard a commotion in the tall pines in the woods above the Rock. We climbed up the steep bank behind the rock and ran into the woods to investigate. We got there just in time to see several crows making noisy conversation in the pine trees above us. Then we saw that one of the crows seemed to be in trouble. He was flopping from branch to branch and falling closer to the ground with each flop.

Then I suddenly realized it was a young crow and he could not yet fly even though he seemed to have all the feathers necessary for the job. We chased him about briefly and I finally cornered him under a small bush and caught him with both hands. My first thought was to return him to his nest. I spotted the nest high up in one of the pine trees, but I realized that it would be impossible to climb fifty feet of pine tree with the closest branch thirty feet above the ground with no climbing equipment.

Our original intent was to take him home and raise him until he could get about on his own, but he became almost a member of the family after a while. I built a cage about four feet by four feet square and about six feet high with a perch for him to sit on. The cage was covered with regular chicken wire. I decided to name him "Blacky"; another bit of original thinking.

Blacky settled into his new home with no problems. He actually seemed to enjoy not having to forage for food. Feeding a crow is no problem. They will eat just about anything, including your fingers until they get to know you.

Blacky seemed determined to learn his version of the human language to some degree. After he had been with us for a few weeks, he did not make the usual cawing sounds his brother crows made. If he saw a person walking by the house, he called to them with a strange sounding, "Wahhh, wahhh, wahhhhh!" The person would usually look towards the sound and as likely or not, see us rather than the crow and give us a dirty look and keep on moving away from those weird sounding guys.

Another rather annoying habit he had was to imitate dogs early in the morning. I don't know which one started the arguments; mammal or fowl, but they would wake me up before I really wanted to be awake at times. The dogs would go, "Rowf, rowf, rowf!" That was followed by Blacky's, "Roww, roww, rowww!" I don't know what "Roww, roww, rowww" translates into in dog language, but it must have been very offensive, because the next thing you knew, most of the dogs within hearing distance of Blacky were hurling insults back at him.

If Blacky did not like you, it was better to stay a good distance from his cage. He could; let us say, hurl anal projectiles through the wires of his home with amazing accuracy. I heard a friend of mine yell an expletive one day and went to see what was wrong. He had decided to tease Blacky by pushing him off his perch with a long stick. Blacky decided to teach him some manners by painting the front of his shirt white. Before joining the Navy in 1957, I sadly gave Blacky to my grandfather. He was the one wild pet I had that actually seemed to enjoy civilization.

CHAPTER TWELVE

The Fine Art of Fly Fishing

A S YOU CAN tell from the way this narrative is going, fly-fishing was not one of our strong points in our formative years. We had no fly rods, lines, leaders or even flies; unless you count the feathers on the triple hooks of the few spinners we had, as flies. That type of gear was expensive, even in those days. That is not to say I did not admire those sportsmen I read about in Field & Stream and Outdoor Life. Many times I would dream of being on one of those magnificent streams in Alaska or out west or up in Canada. I could picture myself gracefully casting a fly to a rising Rainbow Trout or one of those beautiful Dolly Vardens in the high country of Montana or Wyoming or wherever those exotic trout reside.

But it was not to be, at least in this stage of our lives. In later years I learned to use a fly rod properly but I never had the urge to tie flies except once and that was in my early years.

There is a time in the very early spring, before the suckers run up Johnson Brook and just after the ice leaves the Cove that fishing is in limbo. The open water is there to tease you with the false promise that maybe you could catch a fish, but deep inside you know the conditions are not quite right until a little later in the spring.

I was always there, waiting and observing each day, hoping against hope the fishing would come earlier this spring than it had in previous years. On this particular day, I was walking the shoreline along the Little Cove from the brook to the pine grove. The ice was still in the Little Cove but it had melted away from the shore about three or four feet. I could see schools of tiny shiners swimming in the weedy waters between the ice cover and the shore. This part of the Cove was the prime breeding ground for the Pickerel. After the ice melted, there were many weeds and small bushes that grew out into the shallow, warmer waters. It was the perfect place for the Pickerel to lay their sticky clutches of eggs among the submerged branches.

I kept walking around the shore until I reached the main part of the Cove, then I climbed up the bank and continued my walk to the mouth of the Cove and the river. About half way to the Cove's mouth, there was a group of White Birches growing at the bottom of the bank. They leaned gracefully out over the water, pointing at the small island near the middle of the Cove. Each spring they leaned toward the water more and more as the current from Johnson Brook washed away the soil at their roots.

I had always liked the view from this spot and stopped once again to admire it. From here you could see the entire Cove and look down into the Little Cove to where it curved around and bent toward the mouth of Johnson Brook. The water was particularly high this spring and had completely surrounded the area that we called the Big Island. The bank of the Pine Grove at this point is facing almost directly south. The warmth of the noonday sun made this a good place to sit and contemplate life or whatever young boys my age contemplate, so I sat down to enjoy the view.

The sun felt good after the icy cold of the past winter. I made a silent wish the rest of the snow and ice would suddenly disappear and summer would miraculously be there. Needless to say, my wish was not granted; the ice was still in the Little Cove and the level of the water flowing slowly by did not drop. As I watched the water under the birches, I saw a slight movement. At first I thought it was a submerged weed waving in the current. I cautiously moved down the bank for a closer look.

Wow, I thought, *part of my wish has been granted!*

There in the water under the trunk of the lowest birch was a large Pickerel! As I stared closer still, I could make out the dark forms of one or two more that were deeper down in the water.

They must have been gathering, waiting as I was for the ice to melt in the Little Cove so they could get on with what they were supposed to do in the spring of the year. I didn't care what their amorous intentions were. All I knew was the itch I suddenly felt was not a black fly or mosquito bite; the fishing bug had bitten me!

I hurried home to see what I had available to start the fishing season with. A quick inventory of the tobacco can that held my fishing gear showed my supply of hooks was nearly depleted. *Nearly* was the wrong word. All I could find was one short shanked hook with the point broken off. I was almost in tears. There was a big fish waiting and I had no way to catch him. This was the worst situation any fisherman could find himself in.

Maybe, I thought, I could make a hook. That shouldn't be too hard. After all, a hook is nothing more than a piece of bent wire with a point on it. This should be easy. All I needed was a piece of wire. I finally found a piece that in its previous life had held together a bundle of cedar shingles. It was close to what I imagined to be the right gauge.

I got my father's pliers out and proceeded to bend the wire into a hook shape. It looked to be about a number four in size. I wrapped the end that was to be the eye around a nail and snipped the end off as close to its shank as I could. Then I filed a sharp point on the business end. It had no barb, much like my old sucker spear. I tried it out by pulling the point against a piece of wood. I was dismayed to see the hook start to straighten out.

Then I remembered an ad I had seen for some Norwegian hooks; Mustad, if I remember correctly. The ad stated that these hooks were stronger because they had flattened out the cross section of the wire by pressing it flat. That was supposed to make the wire stronger. I thought that might be the answer to my little dilemma, so I got a hammer and laid the hook on a flat piece of tire spring I had. I pounded gently on the hook until it was about half of its original thickness.

This worked out beautifully. It gave enough strength to the hook so it did not straighten out as quickly as before. Maybe that would be all I needed. It was the ugliest hook I had ever seen, but it looked as if it had been born with the killer instinct in it.

That solved half the problem before me; the other half being bait. It was too cold for insects to be out and the ground was still frozen too much to dig for worms. That meant I must try something artificial. The most obvious thing was a fly of some sort. But what was I to use? The sum total of my entire fly tying gear was zero. I had no feathers, hackle, hair or anything else with which to tie a fly.

Just about that time, my friend Stinky the skunk came to my rescue. Stinky was just loaded with beautiful, long black and white fur. He was the perfect candidate to contribute material for the cause. I caught up with him, and with the assistance of my mother's scissors, I snipped off some three inch tufts of black and white fur from his tail. He hardly looked the worse for wear.

I tied the skunk fur to the hook with some black cotton thread I found in the drawer of my mother's sewing machine. I put the black fur on top and white fur below. With the fur dressing tied onto the hook, it didn't look bad at all, I thought. A fur coat always improves one's looks you know. I painted the black thread head with some of my mother's red fingernail polish, let it dry, and I was ready for some fishing action.

Luckily, I did have one steel leader left and I tied it to the line and attached the Simpson Skunk Special to it. All this had taken up most of the afternoon, so I was in a hurry to get back to The Cove and try my new creation on one of those Pickerel. I rushed to that same spot in The Cove as fast as my legs could carry me. By now it was getting to be late in the afternoon. Shadows covered the spot under the overhanging birches and I could not see any signs of the fish. My high spirits sank at the thought they might have gone for good.

Well, I thought, *I might as well try a cast or two seeing as how I'm here.*

I sneaked down the bank as far as I dared and stopped. My heart was pounding and my hands shook a little as I worked some line out for my first cast. It would not be a real cast as such. The bank prevented a back cast, and besides, the telescoping steel rod was a far cry from a bamboo fly rod. Also, there was no floating fly line or gut leader, either. I guessed that the under handed flip of the Simpson Skunk Special about fifteen feet out into the water could be forgiven by the fishing gods.

The skunk fly sank out of sight quickly as the wire leader pulled it down into the darkening depths beneath the birches. I gave it a jerky, quick retrieve, hoping to imitate a wounded minnow. At the end of the retrieve, I lifted the fly from the water, a little disappointed that nothing had followed it. But that's just one cast, I thought. The next cast was a few feet farther out and I began the retrieve almost immediately to prevent the fly from sinking as deeply as the previous cast. As it neared the shore, I thought that I had perceived a movement in the depths below the fly. I did not lift the fly from the water, but moved it around in small, erratic circles at the surface. Then I saw it! A large pickerel was slowly rising up to the surface; his eyes focused on the fly. My spirits sank again as he just as slowly sank back into invisibility once more.

At least I know he's there, I thought.

I cast again to about the same spot as with the last cast and tried the same type of retrieve. This time I stopped the retrieve a rod's length from the shore and repeated the erratic circle routine again. This time he did not pull his sneaky fish ploy but shot out of the depths and the fly disappeared into his toothy mouth in an instant! This type of strike took me by surprise and I almost forgot to set the hook.

I recovered from my surprise and set the hook with a firm pull but not too strongly. Remembering how the homemade hook had straightened out so easily before, I was afraid to set the hook as I would normally have done with a store bought one. The Pickerel made a characteristic dive for the bottom and I let him go without too much pressure on the line. He made several more such charges and appeared to be tiring. Finally I worked him carefully to the surface and started to ease him towards me. He lay in the water near the shore and I stepped to the water's edge and pulled him to me.

As I reached for him, he saw me and leaped, splashing water into my face and he dove for the bottom again. For a brief moment, I thought he had gotten away. But the momentary slack in my line was taken up quickly as he headed away and the battle resumed again. The second half of the cautious battle didn't last as long as the first half. He tired quickly and I brought him to the shore at my feet again.

I reached into the water and grasped him firmly behind his head. After a quick trip up the bank to the pines, I laid him on the ground and opened his mouth to remove the hook. The hook almost fell out by itself, and I saw that it had been re-shaped into an "L" instead of the hook shape I had made. I was very lucky to have landed him. My cautious playing of the battle had saved the day for the Simpson Skunk Special. He was over twenty inches long, a very respectable size for a Pickerel in The Cove. But, I was more proud of the fact that I had caught him on a fly with the help of my old buddy, Stinky.

CHAPTER THIRTEEN

On the River at Last!

THERE WERE ONLY two of our neighbors who owned boats on the Penobscot River between the Cove and the Veazie dam. One was Charles Doughty, and the other was a lady by the name of Maude Folsom who lived next door to my grandfather at Eddington Bend. Eventually, when we got a little older and braver, or maybe a little more desperate to expand our horizons, we asked them if we could use their boats. Mrs. Folsom, who knew me well enough from seeing me at my grandfather's house or possibly because I only charged her twenty-five cents to mow her lawn, told me one day I could use her boat to go fishing if I wanted to.

If I wanted to! Want was a very mild verb to describe my urge to get on that river. In fact, I don't think there were any words in the English language with enough power in them to describe that urge. I felt as if I was floating already as I retrieved the oars from her garage and walked to where the boat was tied up on the shore. The boat was a wooden, flat-bottomed rowboat about twelve or fourteen feet long. It was painted white with green trim. A boat of this type is a very safe and stable craft and nearly impossible to capsize. In other words, it was an absolutely perfect craft for a new sailor such as me to use for his first real solo journey on the Penobscot River.

It was also much less of a threat to my life than my cardboard and wax creation of past years.

I laid the oars in the boat and untied the rope that was holding the boat a captive of the shore. I stepped one foot into the bow of the boat and gave the craft a shove away from the shore with the other foot. It slowly and quietly slid out from the shore stern first, through the lily pads and weeds. I took my place on the rower's seat and slid the oars into the oarlocks. I felt as if the birds were singing more sweetly than before and the swallows seemed to be sweeping down to the river's surface to greet me on my maiden journey. The bullfrogs were croaking hoarse good byes to me from the shore as the boat and I drifted away from our shore-bound captivity. I felt a strange sense of freedom that I had never felt before. That sense of freedom has never left me and is enjoyed by me to this day each time I get into a canoe or boat and head off to a new adventure by myself.

I had never rowed a boat before, but I was confident it was not going to take me long to get the hang of it. It was a little awkward at first until I established a certain rhythm. I found the hard part was making sure the boat kept heading in the direction that you wanted it to go. You are facing toward the back of the boat as you row and I was constantly turning my head to correct the course I had set.

By the time I had rowed the mile or so to the cove, I was handling the boat fairly well. It was almost as if I had possibly done this before in another life. I kept the boat on a straight course by watching the wake behind it. A straight wake meant a straight course, which required very little correcting. I also discovered that after you got the boat moving at a comfortable rate of speed, that it required very little effort to maintain this speed. That is, if there was no head wind.

From the middle of the river, I could see Diamond rock over my shoulder as I approached the entrance to The Cove. I turned the boat beyond the pine grove and headed into the opening of The Cove, it appeared more beautiful than ever from this new perspective. This was the first time I had ever seen it from near the middle of the river. My previous views had been looking out at the river from inside the bounds of The Cove. When I was finally within the boundaries of The Cove, I had the feeling I was home. It was safe and familiar and comfortable but at the same time, different. Being able to move about so freely and quickly in a boat was much different than being handicapped by the restrictions our rafts had put on me.

I rowed around in The Cove for a while, enjoying my first cruise and then headed back out into the river. I turned the boat downstream. As I passed Diamond Rock, I discovered the water was relatively shallow on this side of the river and another eddy was formed where the great rock protruded out into the current. There were a great many patches of lily pads growing there. I made a mental note to try fishing there at some time in the future.

It was getting late in the day, so I decided to take the boat back to Mrs. Folsom's house. I didn't want to take a chance that she might think I had used it for too long. I rowed the boat back up the river past The Cove and Doughty's Landing, and then past Mr. Fogg's store located beyond the Grange Hall and pulled into the shore behind the Folsom residence. I leaped ashore and carefully tied the boat to the tree once more and walked up to the house with the oars over my shoulder. I put them back in the garage and thanked her for the use of the boat.

I wanted to ask her if I could use the boat again sometime but was almost afraid she might say no, so I didn't. As I started to leave, she called to me and said, "You can use it whenever you would like when I'm home."

The words had filled my ears like beautiful music and I felt as if I were ten feet tall and weighed but ten pounds. I thanked her again and ran most of the mile to our house to tell Trevor the wonderful news. At last, we had a way to explore the waters of the Penobscot between the dams.

Not wanting to appear too anxious, I waited a few days before I approached Mrs. Folsom again for the use of her boat. With her approval, my brother and I and our fishing gear were soon out on the river in her boat. We decided we would row up to the Veazie dam, seeing as how this was an area that we were unfamiliar with. We rowed upstream on the east shore until the current from the waters rushing over the dam was too much to row against. Pulling the boat up onto the rocky shore a hundred yards or so below the dam, we walked upstream to the area near the fishway.

After climbing up the bank to the top of the dam, we had a wonderful view across the river to the Bangor Hydro Electric plant on the Veazie shore. We could see downstream to where the river made a sharp turn to the west and headed for the dam in Bangor. It was relatively early in the year and there was much water roaring over the dam and at times you had to shout to communicate.

There was a sign on the shore near the boat stating, "No fishing within 100 feet of the fishway." Fishing near the fishway was not on our minds at this time. We were just curious. We walked down the concrete fishway to its end and looked down. It did not seem possible to me that any fish could swim into the torrent pouring forth. We changed our minds about not fishing and decided to try our luck anyway in spite of the sign and baited our hooks with our favorite fish killers; garden worms. I cast a short way out into the current and let the sinker pull the line to the bottom. To my surprise, it didn't take too long for me to feel the familiar tug of a fish hitting the worm. I set the hook and the fish headed downstream.

After you have fished for a few years, you can tell with a reasonable degree of certainty what fish you have hooked by the way it resists the line. I knew right away that I had hooked into an eel. There was a hard, steady pull and the line had a regular pendulum-like back and forth rhythm caused by the way an eel resists the hook. It does so with a steady back and forth, snake-like motion.

I have never liked to catch eels because of another physical characteristic possessed by them. They are covered with a heavy coating of thick slime. This in itself is not too bad, but they also have a strong tendency to roll up on the line and make a slimy, messy tangle of eel and line. In those days, we could not afford to buy new hooks all the time, so we had to deal with this problem. We could not just cut the line above the mess and let the eel go about his business; we needed to save the hook.

Eels have small, fine teeth and there isn't much danger of them drawing too much blood if they bite, but they also have jaws like a pit bull. When they clamp them onto something, they don't like to let go. I usually got my hook back by putting my foot firmly on the eel behind its head and hoped that it was just lip-hooked to make for a relatively easy retrieval of the hook. Even then, you usually had eel slime on your shoe and sometimes around your ankle when a larger specimen pretended to be a python and wrapped itself around your leg. After I got my hook back, I would give the eel a swift kick and send him back into the water. Fortunately for eels, they are very tough fish and being manhandled in this way doesn't seem to faze them at all.

We eventually solved the eel problem by using bobbers on the line so it would not sink to the bottom where the eels congregated. We caught many species of fish at the east shore of the Veazie dam. There were Smallmouth Bass, sunfish, Yellow Perch, and occasionally, a pickerel. We even caught White Perch at times. They were a surprise to us because at that time, we did not know they were in the river. They are much more associated with lakes and ponds.

One day a year or so later, I was fishing from our favorite spot on top of the fishway when I had a strike that felt different than any other strike that I was familiar with. It was a quick hit as if from a fish that was familiar with fast water. As it fought, I could see flashes of silver in the water as he turned away on some of his short runs. I thought it was probably a big white perch or possibly a very large golden shiner. Finally I brought him to the fishway and lifted him from the water and he flopped at my feet. I grabbed him quickly as he tried to wiggle his way back into the water.

The fish was beautiful bright silver in coloration with only slight hints of light colored spots scattered over its body. Its back was dark and steely. The fins and its general shape showed it to be of the trout or salmon family. It didn't have scales like the salmon or the coloration of a brook trout. He was fifteen inches long and every inch a beauty. I carried it to the top of the fishway and put it in a place where it could not escape and went back to fishing in hopes of catching another one. I fished for an hour or so and caught a few bass but no more like him.

I walked back to where I had put the fish and saw that the silver coloration was fading and the familiar coloration of the brook trout was starting to show. Bill Geagan, an outdoor and sports writer for the Bangor Daily News at that time later told me it was most likely a sea run brook trout. Apparently, brook trout that live in waters with access to the ocean also will move out to sea as do salmon and other fish. That was another learning experience for me.

A few years later, I discovered that sea run Brook Trout at the Veazie Dam were not as uncommon as I thought. One evening a few years later, on the opposite side of the river between the dump and the powerhouse, I saw some quick little splashes in the shallow waters about twenty feet from shore. Some fish were definitely feeding on a hatch of some sort as the flies floated down in the current.

I baited a small hook with a worm and cast out to where they were feeding. Fortunately for me, these fish were not finicky eaters preferring only flies. Almost immediately, I had a strike. I brought the fish to shore and found that it was a sea run Brook Trout about ten inches in length. I fished until nearly dark and caught several more; all about the same length. I eventually found that a day or so after a good summer rain, these trout could be caught in that same area. I don't know if that is still true today or not.

After we had our adventure at the dam, we returned down river by way of the opposite shore in Veazie. As we looked up towards a high bank overlooking the far side of the river we had just left, we noticed smoke from a smoldering fire. We returned the boat to Mrs. Folsom with the promise to ourselves that we would investigate the source or that smoke on our next trip up the river.

CHAPTER FOURTEEN

"Where There's Smoke . . ."

DEEP WITHIN MOST of us and probably more so in the depths of those who are living in poverty, is the dream that by some miraculous act of providence, wealth and treasures will befall us. It was no different with me. I can remember dreams where treasure of one kind or another was there and seemed possible to grasp but I would always wake up just before I could get my hands on it.

It has also been said that one man's trash is another mans treasure. In the following parts of this chapter, you will see just how true that statement was to my brother and me and my family.

On the occasions when my brother and I would borrow Mrs. Folsom's rowboat to fish the Veazie dam area, we discovered the other side of the river had some good fishing, also. On the shore of the river a couple of hundred yards below the dam were some large boulders protruding out into the faster current. Smallmouth bass found it was a good idea to hang out in the slower waters behind these boulders. This was because bait fish were there in profusion. If you trolled a streamer fly behind the boat as you rowed by these rocks, more often than not, you would tie into one of these jumping bronze backs.

I always liked to catch smallmouth bass. They, like the Atlantic Salmon, could always be counted on to give a good show when hooked. They are tough fighters and on light tackle will provide an angler with many fond memories as they leap about trying to throw the hook.

Below these rocks, there was another small, gravel beach. Behind the beach was a wooded area that contained many tall white pines. It made a cool, picturesque spot to stop on a hot summer day. We would sometimes put in on this beach if we were tired of rowing around. You could then climb out on the boulders and cast for smallmouths. This was also a good spot to fish on the river bottom with worms for yellow perch, sunfish or eels.

This beach also happened to be just below the place where we had observed smoke high up on the bank on our first boat trip up to the dam. One day while relaxing on this little beach, we decided this would be a good a time to check out the source of that smoke. We entered the wooded area behind the beach and climbed up the bank towards its source. It was not an easy climb because there were many large boulders, fallen trees and blackberry bushes to climb over or through. When we finally got to the top of the bank, we stepped out into an open area and walked toward the smoke.

No two people see things in the same way. I looked at what was before me and thought, *Oh darn, it's nothing but a big dump.* I felt disappointment, even though I had no expectations of anything in particular for the source of the smoke. But, as I said before, one man's trash is another mans treasure. My brother looked at it and then exclaimed with excitement and anticipation in his voice, "Wow! Look at that! It's a *dump!*" For all those moderns among us today; a dump is now known as a landfill.

His enthusiasm prompted me to take another look around and to re-evaluate my previous assessment of this place. We walked about and as we did, I could see that this was not just a dump. It had potential for a lot of fun for two young boys. Before long we were setting up bottles on boxes and throwing rocks at them. It was very satisfying to see them smash into hundreds of pieces and to not hear anyone tell us to stop. Seagulls were the only ones who seemed to object to our play. They did not enjoy having rocks flying by them as they scavenged for a meal in the trash.

It was not long before we found that seagulls and boys were not the only visitors to the dump. If you stood still for a minute or so, you could see small animals scurrying about beneath the debris. There was an occasional red squirrel or chipmunk but rats were doing most of the scurrying. Not just ordinary rats, but very large rats! That didn't bother me too much. I had seen rats before, even in our house on occasion. It looked as if most of this rat population had sores on their bodies. I don't know if this is common among the rat population of dumps, but in the Veazie dump, the rats were a very sorry looking bunch in general.

Looking more closely about the dump, I found old books and magazines strewn about. To me, *this* was the real treasure. It was hard for me to imagine anyone actually throwing away a perfectly good issue of "Field & Stream" or "Outdoor Life" or "True, the Man's Magazine" if they were only a few months old. After all, they cost twenty-five cents apiece! I found a box just the right size and started to salvage as many as I could that weren't soggy from rain or didn't smell too badly from the smoke or the other dump odors. I even found a ceramic shoe about two inches long and several issues of "Modern Romance" magazine for my mother.

The fire had done a reasonably good job of turning trash to ash that day, so we took our new found treasures with us and headed back through the woods to the river and the boat. I had noticed the dump was not on fire all the time, but was burned only periodically. With this in mind, I made up my mind to come back at another time between the periodic burnings to see what the good citizens of Veazie were going to contribute to our cause.

We made many fishing trips to the dam that summer. Learning how to fish a new area is always a time consuming project. Sometimes it can be as easy as using your eyes to locate schools of baitfish or seeing fish constantly jumping and feeding in a certain area. Other times, you can get good information from other fishermen as to what is biting on what bait or in which area they are feeding. Most of the time, it was just good old-fashioned trial and error. Just because an area looked "fishy" did not necessarily mean there were fish there. There were other times when fish were in areas that made us wonder why they were there at all.

After many of these combination fishing and exploration trips to the dam, we would make a side trip to the dump. As I said in an earlier chapter, the dump is remembered by me as a combination antique store, shopping mall and recreation center for good reasons. As one example of it being an antique store, we had found an old hand-wound Victrola record player that was in nearly new condition. We carted it home in the boat and used it for many years after. I had found several books on area history that had been published fifty or a hundred years before. In later years they would be valued at hundreds of dollars. It seemed in the late forties and throughout the fifties, no one valued the past as we do today.

As a shopping mall, the dump was years ahead of its time. Back in those days, there was no such thing as shopping centers. You went to the butcher store if you wanted meat, to the bakery if you wanted good bread or to a clothing store if you wanted clothes. The closest thing to a super market was the local A&P or IGA stores. You might be able to pick up something other than food there, but it was unlikely. The dump had it all if you weren't too fussy. But the very best thing about the Veazie dump was this; everything was free! You did not have to part with a penny for anything you found. It was wonderful!

One time we found a whole box of records. A beer distributor apparently threw them away because when we got them home, they turned out to be beer commercials for Pabst Blue Ribbon Beer. The soothing strains of, "What'll you have? Pabst Blue Ribbon; what'll you have? Pabst Blue Ribbon; what'll you have? Pabst Blue Ribbon . . . Pabst Blue Ribbon Bee-ee-er!" sounded throughout the house from our "new" Victrola for many days after that.

At the same time, we also found many heavy cardboard cutouts of the brewery's bottled products. We had cutouts of every bottle of beer that the distributor sold. Our father, who was an alcoholic, took offense to all of these colorful cutouts that covered my bedroom walls and made me take them all down. At the time, I could not figure out what made him so hostile. I only wanted to lend a little color to the drab walls of my room. In later years when I became a little wiser, I figured out what his problem was all by myself.

The summer soon ended and Mrs. Folsom put her boat up for the winter. I was sad to see this happen because in my mind, there was still another month or so where we could still use the boat before the river froze over. We could still fish at the Veazie dam if we wanted to by walking up Route 9 to Eddington Bend. The dam could then be reached by a short dirt access road by way of Route 178 that followed along the Penobscot River. It wasn't the same as getting to the dam by way of the river, but the walk was not too bad for our young legs. It did put a temporary halt to the dump excursions, though.

Fall came and went and the cold Maine winter set in. Fishing went out with the incoming snow and cold weather. But with the coming of cold temperatures, came the freezing of the river. The waters between the dams moved at a comparatively slow rate as the river widened below the Veazie dam. This allowed the waters of the Penobscot to freeze over to a thickness that would allow skating and walking on the river. Along with the ice and snow came the possibility of more adventure. With the Penobscot covered with a sheet of ice, it was now possible to cross the river on the ice and to walk up the other side to the Veazie dump.

Trevor was always a little more adventurous and daring than me, so it was not too much of a surprise to me when he came home one day and said that he had been up to the dump. I did not think the river ice was strong enough to support a more timid soul such as me, but he convinced me it was. We went down to the river the next day and I took a look at the ice for myself. Near the shore the ice was possibly four or five inches thick, but as we got nearer to the middle of the river, it thinned out to around two inches or so in places. The current flowed faster under the ice here than it did near the shore.

It made me nervous to walk over relatively thin ice that made cracking noises as it expanded. It seemed to me as if it was about to swallow me up and I started at any unusual sound. Looking down and seeing the waters moving by under my feet did not help me feel any more secure. Occasionally a small stick or piece of debris would float by under my feet and I could almost visualize my own face staring up through the ice with a frozen stare on it; mouth agape in horror.

The ice gradually got thicker as we got beyond the middle of the river and my pounding heart slowed to normal. After that, it was an easy walk up the west shore to the dump. I tried not to think about the return trip over the same crossing. When we got to the dump, it was business as usual. We rummaged about; broke our usual quota of bottles and terrorized the rat population. After playing about for awhile, we headed back down the frozen river to where we had crossed over. On our return crossing, I found a long tree branch and took it with me as I walked. I thought if I did fall through the ice, the branch might give me a fighting chance for survival. My worries were unfounded and we both arrived home safely.

As the winter progressed, the ice got thicker and safer. Over the river and through the woods to the Veazie dump we'd go. Trips to the dump made the long winter days pass a little faster and more enjoyably. Aside from snow forts and snow houses and snowball fights, there wasn't a lot to do in the winter except to try to keep warm and dry.

One afternoon I heard Trevor come in the back door and the sound of packages being dumped onto the kitchen table reached my ears. "Come here and see what I found up at the dump," he yelled to my mother and sisters and me.

We all walked into the kitchen and stared in amazement at what was on the table. He had put a pile of packaged cookies on the table the likes of which I had never seen except in a store. We had seen packages of cookies at the dump before, but they had always been broken open and the rats and seagulls were feasting on them. That the packages may have been intact upon arrival had never occurred to us.

Trevor explained that while he was there, a truck from a bakery distributor in Veazie had come and dumped the goodies. After the truck had left, he had gone over to see what they had thrown out. It was every poor boys dream . . . cookies! Store bought cookies were a rare luxury to our family. Necessities such as potatoes, flour, lard and salt pork were much more important. Occasionally, we would get hamburger or cold cuts, but cookies; almost never.

Needless to say, we did not question the Cookie Gods about this little miracle. We soon overcame our instinct to not eat something that came out of a dump. After all, hadn't Trevor gotten to them before rats and seagulls had scavenged them? Believe me when I tell you, they tasted as good to us as if we had purchased them from the store. We later figured out that at around three-thirty on Thursday afternoons, the truck came and dumped outdated bakery goods collected from customers' stores in the area. Whenever we could, we kept our busy calendar open on Thursday afternoons after that.

Maybe now you can see why something as common as a town dump in Veazie, Maine played an important role to my family and me in my youth. If we had not seen the plume of smoke rising from that spot, we probably would never had gone up to that particular spot and would have missed all the adventures that we had there; not to mention the cookies!

CHAPTER FIFTEEN

High Finances

THIS CHAPTER MAY not sound as if it has much to do with The Cove and the river, but I'm going to include it only as a lesson in how to turn nothing into something if you are desperate enough . . . and believe me we were desperate at times. Also, in order to make money this way, we *did* have to cross over Johnson Brook and walk by The Cove, so *there* is the tie-in.

There were no MacDonald's or Burger Kings around back in the good old days. A kid had to do real work to make money, such as mowing lawns, picking beans or potatoes in season, or other sweaty, labor-intensive type jobs. There were jobs available in grocery stores bagging groceries and taking them out to the customers' cars. You might even get a tip for that. But those jobs usually fell to the high school students who had the best grades and whose teachers had a little political pull with the storeowners.

A two-mile long paper route with thirty-three customers at a penny a paper and two lawns at twenty-five cents apiece helped to buy a few clothes for school in my later years. It wasn't until I was old enough to get a job in a shoe factory in my late teens that I ever had any sort of real money in my pocket.

One of the saving graces of living in Maine back in those days was the deposit on beverage bottles. The purpose of a bottle deposit back in the forties and early fifties had nothing to do with the re-cycling efforts of today. It was to get used bottles back to the beverage companies for cleaning and re-use. I'm presuming they were washed and sterilized before reuse. These bottles were stronger than the non-returnable type due to their heavier construction.

The other kind, being lighter in construction and apparently not strong enough for refilling, offered no deposit. We couldn't care less about those. The lust in our hearts was only for the refillable ones with a price on their heads. The quart size bottles were worth a nickel to us. The smaller size bottles of about twelve ounces or more had a value to us of three cents. The more common size; the eight or ten ounce soft drink bottles, brought us only two cents each.

That doesn't sound like a lot, but back in those days, a candy bar cost a nickel and the movies were only twelve cents if you were under the age of twelve, or twenty-five cents for the unfortunate among us who were over twelve. I was small for my age and got into the movies for twelve cents until I was nearly sixteen years old. I guess there's something good to be said for not eating too high off the hog.

Beer was fifty cents a quart plus five cents deposit, and my father drank quite a bit of beer. If we were careful, we could sneak one of his empties and convert it into a candy bar or a half-pint paper cup of Hershey's Vanilla or Chocolate Ice Cream up the river at Mr. Fogg's store, which we ate with the flat wooden spoon provided. My father kept pretty close tabs on his bottles because the five cent deposit meant that if he returned eleven bottles, it was almost like getting another bottle of beer free.

There were, and probably still are, those in this world who care nothing about the deposit on a bottle, and I would like to thank them *all* at this time. If those fortunate people were driving along in a car and the bottle they were drinking from became empty; out the window it went. I loved those litterbugs! I still have a soft spot in my heart for them. Because of people like that, my brother and I could walk into town with a paper bag in our hands and finance a trip to the movies or buy fishhooks or a line. (There! *Another* tie-in to the river and The Cove!)

I would walk the three miles into town on one side of the road and Trevor would be on the other side, and if all went well, we would have the bags full before we got to Perkins Variety Store in Brewer to cash them in.

If not, we would split the few cents we got and hitchhike home to search again some other day.

There were four movie houses in Bangor back in the forties and fifties. The elite one was the Bangor Opera House on Main Street. That was where the Disney productions usually played, but they did not have double features. The Bijou was located on Exchange Street and was on a par with the Opera house. My favorite theater was the Park Theater on the corner of Exchange and State Street. And there, lurking at the bottom of the movie barrel, was the Olympia Theater. Back in the really old days I think it was called the Nickelodeon, but it was known affectionately by all of us youngsters as the Rat Hole.

The Rat Hole was aptly named. On the few occasions when it was showing a movie I just had to see, there actually were rats running around by your feet looking for dropped candy or popcorn. At times you might even see a few running around on the stage. I used to keep my feet up on the seat where they couldn't run over them; or as I feared, up my pant legs!

The Park Theater was my favorite because it seemed to cater to us younger people. It was cleaner by far than the Olympia and was definitely not as scary when the lights went down. Plus . . . it showed double features on weekends of all the very best of the B movies, as we call them today. One movie was usually a western and the other could be a comedy, science fiction, detective or horror movie. Besides the two movies, there were always two cartoons, a short subject, a serial such as Flash Gordon or Rocket Man, the newsreels, and the coming attractions. Talk about getting your twelve cents worth!

On occasion, they would have a two-hour cartoon extravaganza starting at ten o'clock on Saturday morning and running until noon. After the cartoons were over, you had to clear out of the theater before the regular features began. Of course, that meant you would have to pay again to re-enter the theater. Some of the older, bolder boys would hide behind the stage curtains until the features started and then sneak out and take a seat as soon as the house lights went down.

At one time in our young lives; a very *short* time, my older sister and I got a twenty-five cent a week allowance. That beat traipsing all the way into Brewer searching for bottles on the sides of the road. The bus; Cyr Bus Line from Old Town, went by our house on North Main Street three times a day; early in the morning, around noon time, and about four-thirty in the late afternoon. After arriving in Bangor at the terminal on the corner of Central and Hammond Streets, it picked up passengers and made the reverse trip past our house and back to Old Town. The last bus of the day left the terminal at 5:00 p.m.

The fare was five cents one way to Bangor. That meant ten cents of our quarter went for the bus fare to and from Bangor, twelve cents went for admission to the movies and that left us with three cents burning a hole in our pockets.

J. J. Newberry's store was located about halfway up Main Street between the bus station and the Opera House. They sold candy, fancy crackers and bulk pretzel sticks in the candy department. I always bought the pretzel sticks because they were sold for nine cents a pound. We could buy a third of a pound of pretzels with our three cents. That's a lot of pretzels. We munched on the pretzels from a plain, brown paper bag on the way home on the bus. With a little luck, there would be some left over for the next day.

It may sound as if the Simpsons had it really bad in those days. While we didn't have new clothing or an allowance most of the time and we nearly froze to death in the winter and our diet wouldn't meet with the government's approval, I suspect that we may have gotten more fun out of life than most of our friends who were better off than we were. Even though times were rough, there were many interludes of happiness in our lives; *if* you were satisfied with small pleasures. When you are poor, it's amazing how small pleasures grow and become large ones.

CHAPTER SIXTEEN

Riding the River in Style!

WHAT COULD BRING more pleasure to a young man than being on a body of water that is loaded with fish, with a fishing rod in one hand and a plentiful supply of bait or lures in the other? The obvious answer to that question is . . . doing it with *style!*

Trevor and I had always managed to come up with solutions to all our piscatorial crises, one way or another. But wouldn't it be nice if we had the ultimate craft to ply the waters of the Penobscot or the Cove? In the State of Maine, that ultimate craft would have to be a canoe. Even in the fifties, canoes were relatively expensive in comparison to a rowboat. A canoe seemed to be an unattainable dream far beyond our meager means.

But, times passes and we grew older and, eventually, we got real jobs. Just about all of our friends' first jobs were in the shoe factories of Bangor. Shoes and paper were the major products of central Maine in those days. Nearly every city or town of any size had a factory, or factories, that manufactured shoes and/or paper. So it was that my first real job that paid me a regular salary was in the Viner Brothers shoe factory on good old Hancock Street in the City of Bangor.

You are not going to get rich at an "entry level" job in a shoe factory, even today; if you can even find a shoe factory in the United States anymore. At that time, the minimum wage was seventy-five cents an hour. To me, that seemed to be a small fortune! However, believe it or not, a single person could survive on seventy-five cents an hour in those times. You could actually rent a room, buy your clothes from the Salvation Army store, feed yourself and still be able to finance a cheap automobile. I mean, *really* cheap!

I had two dreams after I got that job. Dream number one was to get a car, and dream number two was to get a canoe; or was it the other way around? Even today, if I was alone and living in Maine, those would *still* be my first two priorities. After all, man does not live by bread alone! Fish sandwiches are much better!

My first dream came true a few months after starting my new job. My cousin, "Sib" Orcutt, and I were wandering around the back lot of the Sullivan Ford dealership on outer Hammond Street in Bangor, and there it was! A black, 1941 Plymouth business coupe in excellent condition! I felt it call to me as I walked by and I answered the call and walked over to it.

I thought the price was a little too high; after all, A hundred and twenty-five dollars didn't grow too quickly on the Simpson money tree. And besides, most cars of that vintage were going for about a hundred dollars at that time. This car was special, though. The engine had just been rebuilt and was painted a gleaming silver color. When you started that silver engine and let it idle, you couldn't even hear it run or feel any vibrations from that smooth running engine. I just had to have it. Even though I hadn't bothered to get a driver's license, I drove it home that very day.

Dream number two came true shortly after that in the form of a terse classified ad in *The Bangor Daily News*. "Canoe for sale. $10.00." It gave the address of a hardware store in Brewer. The ad had been running for a couple of days, so I almost didn't bother to check it out. After all, a ten-dollar canoe probably wasn't in very good condition. Besides, if it was in good shape, it would probably have been sold long before I could get down there, anyway. I tried to talk myself out of looking at that canoe, but in the end I thought, *What the heck! Why not take a look at it. If it's not in too bad of a condition, I might be able to fix it up.*

I drove the three miles to Brewer and inquired if they still had the canoe that was advertised in the paper. Indeed they did. It was stored upstairs. The fact that they still had it made me pretty sure it couldn't be much of a canoe, but I followed the man up the stairs for a look. After all, I was there, wasn't I?

When we reached the second floor, I saw a dark green, twenty-foot White brand canoe resting on its thwarts on some supports hanging from the ceiling. I looked around for the canoe that was advertised in the paper. "Where is the canoe you have for sale?" I inquired; not believing that this could be the one.

The man pointed at the twenty-foot White and answered, "There she is, young man." My heart did a few flip-flops and my eyes opened wide. I could feel myself getting faint! It was love at first sight! For the uninitiated, the White Canoe Company built some of the finest cedar and canvas canoes in the world at that time. The Old Town Canoe Company, located in the same town, was a competitor and built canoes of equal quality.

I checked out the condition of the canoe and still couldn't believe that this could be the one advertised. "Ten dollars, huh?" I said, trying to appear nonchalant; praying that there had been no typographical errors on the part of the *Bangor Daily News*, like misplacing a decimal point or something of that order.

"Yup. That's what he wants. It's taking up too much space and he wants it out of here."

I whipped out my ten dollars and handed it to the man. My mother raised no fools. Now the problem of getting a twenty-foot canoe home was upon me. I had no boat racks, but fortunately the guy who had my money also had the solution to that little problem. He rolled up two burlap gunny sacks and laid them across the roof of my car and told me we would just lay the canoe on these and tie the front and back of the canoe to the car's bumpers. This system worked so well that I used it until I sold the canoe to my uncle, Lloyd Mann, for twenty dollars a few years later when I joined the Navy.

Before I left, the man told me to wait a few moments. He went back upstairs and came down with two canoe paddles. One was a six footer and the other a five and a half footer. *Wow!* I thought, *All this and paddles, too, for only ten dollars!* I couldn't believe my good fortune. (Those same paddles would sell today (2006) for more than two-hundred dollars and a comparable twenty foot guide canoe from Old Town Canoe would cost in the neighborhood of five thousand dollars!) Times do change, don't they?

I drove home with my brand new, used canoe secured firmly to the top of my car. When I pulled into my driveway and got out to give my prize a closer look, I realized at that moment how big a twenty-foot long canoe really is. I had help putting the canoe on top of the car, but now I was on my own. That was when I found out how *heavy* a twenty-foot canoe really is.

I was a really skinny guy back in those days. I was five feet nine inches in height, but weighed in at only about a hundred and twenty pounds. All that walking, rowing boats and pushing rafts about on the river and the

Cove helped me out in the muscle department. I was pretty strong for my size. The canoe might have outweighed me by a bit, but I managed to get it off the top of the car by myself. I could actually get the thing balanced on my shoulders and walk with it if need be. I wouldn't have been able to portage very far with it alone, but it wasn't built for that type of canoeing. It was built for big lakes and big loads. Fortunately, there were only a few times when I would require help with it. Most of the time Trevor and I would be using it together. Even if you don't know what you are doing, you can just put a canoe in the water, get in and start paddling. Chances are good that you will instantly find out that if you paddle on one side only, you will start to go around in a circle. Then you find that you have to start switching from side to side in order to keep the craft going in a somewhat straight line. I had seen many a canoeist do just that.

However, I had been in canoes several times before with a guy who really knew how a canoe was to be handled. He had taught me the classic "J" stroke that would keep the canoe on a straight course without switching from side to side with the paddle; the sure sign of the amateur paddler. The "J" stroke got its name from the fact that the blade of the paddle traces a course similar to the letter "J" as it propels the canoe through the water. The paddle is dipped into the water and stroked back close to the gunwales in the usual way, but at the end of the stroke, the blade is feathered edgeways and stroked outward and away from the hull of the canoe. This little variation of the stroke, when practiced and perfected, is the secret of appearing like you know what you are doing in a canoe. It also has the added advantage of keeping the floor of your canoe (and perhaps even a passenger sitting in front of you) dry from switching back and forth with your paddle. Even if you are careful, water dripping from the blade of a paddle will drip onto the floor and possibly splatter onto anything in front of you. This is not harmful to the canoe, but it might be harmful to you; depending on how easily irritated your passenger might get after being wet a few times from your careless paddling.

I managed to get the canoe down to Dean's Landing without breaking my back. Seeing that beautiful canoe setting there on the sandy shore with the Penobscot River in the background was one of the prettiest sights my young eyes had ever seen. You have to be a fisherman to understand; a poor (meaning, monetarily deprived) fisherman. I trudged back up the trail to my car to retrieve the paddles with dreams filling my mind about the adventures ahead of me. My elation knew no bounds. I would at last be able to ride the waters of the Penobscot in real style! What could be better than that?

CHAPTER SEVENTEEN

My First Ride in Style and Other Adventures

NEEDLESS TO SAY, my trip back to the river with paddles in hand took much less time than it did with the canoe on my back. I was so elated that I hadn't paid much attention to the weather. The sun was riding high and the temperature was great, but a wind had sprung up from the southwest and was blowing at a pretty fair clip almost directly up the Penobscot.

I pushed the canoe into the water, climbed in, and sat in the stern seat. A few pushes with the paddle against the sandy bottom and I was underway. The bow was riding a little high, but the length and weight of the canoe kept it fairly flat in the water. Even at that, the wind swung the bow swung around and pointed the canoe in the general direction of upstream. That was okay with me; I wanted to go upstream to the Veazie Dam, anyway.

With the wind at my back, it was no time at all before I found myself across the river and on my way upstream. The shortest way to the Veazie Dam was to edge your way across the river and follow the opposite shore upstream at the Bend until you got there. As I neared the far side of the river where it turns north, I saw my grandfather on the opposite shore at his home at Eddington Bend. I decided that I would cross the river and show him my new canoe. I had been enjoying the canoe to such an extent that I had not noticed that in the very short time I had been paddling that the wind had picked up considerably in strength. The speed of the wind against the current of the river was raising some pretty fair whitecaps. This didn't bother me too much. I knew that a canoe of this size was built for heavy weather and heavy loads. Wind was no problem . . . or so I thought.

What could be simpler than to turn the canoe and head across the river and visit with my grandfather? All I had to do was to widen my expert "J" stroke into a wider straight stroke; maybe with a slight opposite "J" to the tail end of it, and the canoe would turn and I would be on my way across the river. Well, you know what they say about the best laid plans of mice and fishermen! Trying as hard as I could, the canoe would not turn in that direction. The strength of the trailing wind combined with the slightly raised bow of the canoe kept the canoe on a straight course up the river. I tried and tried but to no avail. I was destined to be blown straight up river and into the maw of the waters cascading over the dam! At least, that was the overly dramatic thought that entered my mind.

Inspiration struck me like a lightning bolt. I carefully made my way up the length of that recalcitrant canoe and sat in the forward seat. Facing back to the stern, I started paddling as hard as I was able. The front seat in a canoe is closer to amidships than the rear seat is, and this helped to keep the stern (now the bow) down and helped to prevent the wind from turning the canoe again. Even then, with the wind pushing against me, it was quite a chore to paddle a twenty foot canoe against a strong wind by myself. When I finally made it to the safe haven of the shore by my grandfather's house, I was soaked with sweat and felt as limp as a wet dish rag.

I dragged the canoe onto the shore and walked up to my grandfather's place. He was standing there with a smile on his face. I could see he was trying to suppress a laugh. He just shook his head and said, "I was wonderin' who the damn fool was that would take a canoe out in wind like this. You look like you could use a drink of cold water."

I didn't argue with him. I *was* a damn fool. After that, I paid much closer attention to the weather and how my canoe was loaded before I headed out on a canoe trip by myself; even a short one. If I had been in a lighter canoe, it might have swamped as I tried to turn it, loaded the way it was. A canoe should be trimmed and level in the water. It's almost as important as in an airplane. It's okay to make a mistake as long as you can learn from it, but making a mistake in a canoe can cost you *before* you can learn the lesson. As I said before, I didn't know how to swim.

I left the canoe with my grandfather and walked the mile or so home. The next day, I walked back with my brother and we spent several hours exploring the area around the Veazie dam in the canoe. In spite of its large size, once I got used to it, its stability made it a pleasure to use; with an extra paddle aboard and on windless days, anyway.

*　　*　　*

Back in those years, the men who worked at the Veazie dam knew that later in the year when the fishway at the Bangor dam was open, there were quite a few salmon in the waters below the Veazie dam. We found that to be true, also. One day Trevor discovered a walkway at the base of the powerhouse. It was made of heavy concrete and was about four or five feet away from where the waters flowed from beneath the building. Heavy grating prevented large fish from swimming through and into the waterworks. He saw that there were sometimes many large salmon that would swim up to the grating, lured there by the strength of the current coming from the powerhouse, before working their way back out into the river. Laying on the walkway and looking down into the waters between it and the powerhouse, allowed a good view of whatever fish were swimming into the current below.

One day we pulled the canoe up on the rocky shore below the powerhouse and walked up to the walkway. Trevor had developed a plan that would allow us to possibly dine on salmon that night. We put a large triple hook on the fish line along with a heavy sinker. From below the walkway, the line was cast beneath the walkway and up near the fast flowing current coming through the grating. It was held there by the heavy sinker. Then, with a stick in his hand, Trevor laid down on the walkway and caught the line with the stick and pulled it up to him through the space between the walkway and the powerhouse. Using that portion of the line as you would a hand line, he watched until a suitably large specimen of salmon swam by below him. Swinging the line and hook up against the ill-fated fish's side, he would then give a yank and on occasion, would snag the hook into the salmon's side.

After setting he set the hook, I would reel in the slack as the salmon shot out from under the walkway, and the contest was on. We would then run for the canoe, jump in and head out into the current to fight the fish. I remember one occasion very clearly. The salmon was so large that after we got below the swifter current and into the wider, slower waters below the dam, it actually had enough strength to pull the canoe along with both of us in it. We were downstream by my Grandfather's house at Eddington Bend before that fish tired enough to allow us to get it into the canoe.

We never measured or weighed the salmon we caught back in those days, but I can remember one time when we had caught two salmon in The Cove. We put them into a fifty pound grain sack to carry them home. Both of the salmons' tails protruded from the bag by at least six or eight inches. That meant that they were at least three feet long; possibly longer.

*   *   *

Older now and with a job and a car, my natural world of fishing and learning about nature had opened up considerably. Even though The Cove and the Penobscot River between the dams was still my first love, I could now travel to other places that had only been names on a map. There were many places in Hancock and Washington Counties whose names had always fascinated me. Upper and Lower Sabao, First through Fifth Machias Lakes, Nicatous Lake, Sysladobsis Lake, West Grand Lake; all seemed legendary in my mind.

I had read books by Edmund Ware Smith and had also read the outdoor columns and books of Bill Geagan and longed to visit the places they wrote about. Wheels and paddles now made that possible. But this story is about Mantawassuk; the Cove, so maybe I had better leave those adventures for another time.

There was a little trip that in that big twenty foot canoe I made with a friend of mine and my cousin, Sib Orcutt, that, as I look back on it, I wonder why we even attempted it. At first it seemed like a good idea, but when we finally finished the trip, we were all shaking our heads wondering why we did it.

It started out with a seemingly innocent remark by my cousin Sib. "Why don't we put the canoe in the little brook at the bottom of the hill (on Eastern Avenue below Clewleyville Corners) and paddle all the way down to the Cove?"

Why not, indeed? A quick look at a topographic map of the area seems to show that it might be possible. Other than the fact that this particular little no-name brook was twisting and winding, very shallow in some spots and even had a wire fence or two across it in places, the thought of a trip such as that had much appeal to me.

So it was that one Saturday morning my canoe found itself plying the waters of this no-name brook. From Eastern Avenue, this brook winds its way across an area known as The Flats. The Flats were formed by many floods from this little brook over the millennia and is aptly named. The former farmland of The Flats is, indeed, flat! The biggest problem with this trip was that, until you reached Johnson Brook, some of the curves in this tiny stream were so acute the long canoe couldn't go around them! We had to get out several times and actually pull the canoe over short strips of land and put it back into the brook again. In places, alders grew thickly and formed a canopy over the brook to the point where you actually had to bend down to keep them out of your face. Other places were so shallow that we had to drag the canoe to deeper water. Lewis and Clark had nothing on us!

After what seemed like forever and sweating like pigs, (Do pigs really sweat?) we finally reached Johnson Brook and headed downstream towards the Penobscot River and the Cove. Johnson Brook was a pleasure to be floating on after the taxing trek down no-name. We coasted downstream with minimal paddling until we reached the wooden bridge on the Lambert road. There, we had to get out of the canoe and push it under the bridge and grab it when it when it floated out the other side. The bridge was so low the canoe just cleared its timbers by inches.

Back in the water again, we pressed onward once more. This part of Johnson Brook is wide and flat with a slow current and passes through old hayfields bordered by alders and scattered trees to the west. Its eastern shore is woodland. The curves were very shallow and no problem to navigate at all even with my twenty foot monster. There are Smallmouth Bass and Sunfish here and several species of minnows. On occasion, I had caught a Brook Trout or two in the colder, spring fed spots.

After a half mile or so, we reached the spot where the power line crosses the brook. Here also is where high ledges form a steep drop that is impossible to navigate in any canoe. Our original plan was to portage around this obstacle. We parked the canoe and walked down below the ledges. It was obvious to us that the water was too shallow to allow us to continue on in the canoe. It was mid summer and rocks and ledges were exposed everywhere. If we were ever to make it to the Penobscot, we would have to do it in the spring of the year when there was plenty of depth in the brook.

We were disappointed; but not *too* disappointed. Each of us was tuckered out from the ordeal of that long, long mile down no-name brook.

Right then and there, our plan changed. We decided to paddle back up Johnson Brook to the wooden bridge on the Lambert Road. Then we would leave the canoe, walk the two miles back to our starting point at no-name, drive the car back to the canoe, load it onto the car and call our adventure finished. There were no dissenting votes.

That night, I dreamed that I was a rich man. The first thing I bought with my new wealth was a Jeep and a beautiful green, fifteen-foot fifty pound model Old Town canoe. At fifty-two or three pounds, it was as the weight of a feather to me in comparison to my twenty foot White.

CHAPTER EIGHTEEN

All Good Things Must Come to an End;
Including This Book!

THE TITLE OF this chapter tells it all. All good things; as do bad things, do indeed "come to an end". My brother and I were growing older, we both had jobs now, and with our new mobility, our life on the Penobscot River was entering its final stages. Those stages might not have come about so quickly, but we had a lot of help from Mother Nature back in the mid-fifties in the form of devastating hurricanes, and even more help from environmentalists and the electric companies in the years after that.

According to the records of the National Hurricane Center (NHC), on August 25th of 1954, Hurricane Carol became the first of many large nails driven with mighty force into the coffin of The Cove. Hurricane Carol formed near the Bahamas on that day and slowly moved up the eastern coast of the United States. It missed the south-eastern and mid-Atlantic coastlines by a hundred miles or so, but arrived as a category three storm that hit Long Island and Connecticut with its full fury on the 31st of August of that year. Later that day and the next, it pounded its way into Maine with winds that gusted at over a hundred miles an hour. Block Island had reported one gust that had topped 130 miles per hour.

The winds of a hurricane by themselves are bad enough, but most of the permanent damage in the area of The Cove was caused by the massive amounts of water in the form of torrential rains of ten inches or more in only a few hours that accompanied Carol. Johnson Brook's course was changed in places so drastically that I was never again able to find a particular shaded spot that used to hold Brook Trout on most occasions. So much water roared down its course that when it reached The Cove, half of the area that formed the Point was washed away and re-deposited as a deep gravel bar that reached out to the small island near the center of The Cove.

The flat rock, where I had sought refuge from the "sharks" and where I had watched that little pickerel devour its oversized meal and where the young Bud Simpson had floated along with the clouds, was tipped up on its side and moved closer to the center of The Cove. Those birches that hung precariously over the waters at the base of the pine grove and where I had caught the pickerel with the Simpson Skunk Special had finally been washed away.

The Flats on Eastern Avenue at the foot of the hill at Clewleyville Corners, where my twenty foot canoe began its little journey to the Cove, looked like a large lake for several days after Carol had departed. One of my uncles, Bill York, had driven his car into that no-name brook on the night of the hurricane. I was at my Uncle Earl Orcutt's house on the Clewleyville Road that night. Bill somehow managed to get out of his car without being swept away by the waters roaring down the brook. He told us that he attempted to drive across the bridge because it didn't look as though much water was flowing over it. What he didn't realize was that the bridge was no longer there. It had washed out from the force of the waters. What had appeared to his eyes through the rain and in the dim headlights of his car were not just a few inches of water flowing over a bridge, but water that was six inches higher than the road with no bridge under it.

It seemed as if all the hilly, secondary roads in southern Maine had been washed out. The steeper hills on these roads had become waterfalls and the roads were changed into deeply rutted gorges that resembled rock strewn stream bottoms instead of roads. None of the roads in the Clewleyville area were paved at that time. They were all typical, gravel based country roads and they all suffered the same fate. I was not able to drive my car back to my home on North Main Street in North Brewer for three or four days.

I finally managed to get my car home by a circuitous route. With me driving and my cousin Sib and my friend, Stanley Pluard guiding me by walking in front of the car when necessary, I managed to straddle many deep ruts and navigate the washed out sections. We finally made it to Route 9, a paved road that went by my house, by way of the Nolan, Levensellar and Rooks (formerly, Bagaduce) Roads. It wasn't until then that I was able to walk to The Cove and see the tremendous damage the storm had inflicted upon it. I thought it couldn't be any worse than what I was seeing, but what I didn't know then was that Mother Nature had another surprise in store for me in the not too distant future. She went by the name of Edna.

Less than two weeks later, on September 11th, Hurricane Edna walloped New England with a storm that followed a nearly identical path, but slightly east of Carol's. It followed the coastline instead of going ashore and then went through the New England states and into Canada. The result was much more damage and many more coffin nails for The Cove and Johnson Brook. These two hurricanes by themselves destroyed the character of The Cove and most of our favorite fishing spots. It was as if someone had filled in a third of the area of The Cove at the mouth of Johnson Brook with gigantic loads of gravel, rock and silt. After Edna had done her damage, my favorite flat rock had disappeared. I thought it was probably buried under the latest onslaught of rocks and gravel. It was nowhere to be seen.

These two hurricanes caused more than eighty deaths and over five hundred million dollars in damage before leaving the United States. There is no way to calculate in dollars and cents the damage done to areas like The Cove or to my emotional attachment to the area. To me, it was almost like a death in the family.

And then, a few years later in 1960, came Donna! Donna was another hurricane and she earned the dubious reputation as one of the greatest hurricanes of all time. She was the only hurricane that maintained hurricane force winds for the entire length of her track and plowed into New England still carrying the winds of a category 1 or 2 storm. I would loved to have been there when Donna hit Maine but she arrived there on September the 12th, 1960, almost six years to the day after Edna had her way with The Cove, but by then, I had joined the Navy in 1957, had gotten married, and was stationed in Long Beach, California aboard the U.S.S. Hamul, AD20, waiting to be discharged three months later. I stayed in California from 1960 until my marriage ended in divorce in 1974. During those years, I had made several trips back to Maine. I visited The Cove once or twice, but not to fish. The fishing as I had known it was finished.

The waters still backed up into the remains of The Cove in those days after the hurricanes, but the fill that the hurricanes had washed into it had ruined the fishing and it was much different to me then than in my memories.

After Carol and Edna, the waters from Johnson Brook flowed straight through and around the Little Island instead of flowing to the left of it. The gravel bar that had formed had a few small trees growing on it. It was almost like visiting a badly maintained graveyard. I didn't like what my eyes were seeing.

In 1974, I moved back to Maine and married my present wife, Margo. We eventually bought a house on the Levensellar Road in Holden, Maine, only a ten minute ride from my old hangout. I went fishing and exploring again, but now in Washington and Hancock Counties and not in the remains of The Cove, even though I had to drive by it whenever I drove down North Main Street and into the twin cities of Brewer and Bangor.

The hydro-electric dam between Bangor and Brewer was abandoned by the Bangor Hydro-electric company and fell into disrepair over the ensuing years. It gradually began to fall apart and many breaches appeared in its structure. That dam is no longer in existence now and what remained of The Cove is no longer there because of that. The Cove depended on the backed up waters from the Bangor dam for its very existence. Without the dam, there could be no Cove.

Trevor and I paid a visit to The Cove in 2004. A bronze plaque that used to proudly proclaim that spot as a historic place was no longer standing. It and the granite post it was attached to were difficult to find. We eventually found it; lying on its side and nearly buried in the gravel and weeds growing along the roadside near the bridge over Johnson Brook. I would have thought that the Brewer Historical Society would have taken better care of their monuments. They, of course, had no sentimental attachment to that area. What they knew of The Cove and Johnson Brook were merely the words of history to them or to anyone else who had never shared our experiences there.

We walked down to where The Cove used to be from the bridge at Johnson Brook on North Main Street. It was hard for me to believe what my eyes beheld. The brook now flowed to the left of the former Little Island once more, probably thanks to Hurricane Donna in 1960. The main portion of The Cove where the best fishing for Pickerel, Bass, Yellow Perch and shiners had been was now grown up into a tangled jungle of trees and shrubs. We had a hard time finding the spots where we had found so much joy in fishing and learning about nature.

A walk up into the Pine grove proved a revelation to me. While standing there and trying to look through the trees that had grown up in The Cove, I looked down to where the many tons of debris had filled The Cove all the way to the base of the pine grove. Something caught my eye. Was what I seeing really true? I walked down the bank a ways for a better look. Sure enough; there it was! It couldn't be anything else. The flat rock of my youth was lying there; somewhat askew, but there it was. As near as I could figure, the force of the waters from another hurricane; again, possibly Hurricane Donna in 1960, had exhumed it from its burial place and had sent it to its final (?) resting place completely on the opposite side of The Cove from where it provided me a haven so many years before.

After finding my flat rock, we followed Johnson Brook downstream and to the right a short distance to where it turns sharply to the right and flows into the Penobscot River. When we arrived at the rocky edge of the river, I looked back. Where I was standing, there would have been ten feet of water back when I was young, but now I felt almost as if I were in a wide canyon. The spot that had been The Cove was actually above me.

The head of tide reaches back up the Penobscot now to where it did back in the days when General Waldo kicked the bucket on the 23rd of May in 1759. Trevor and I were there when the tide was out. It seemed strange to be looking *up* at Picked Diamond instead of seeing it from the higher angle of where the surface of the river used to be.

We walked upstream along the river trying to find more familiar spots. The ledges at Doughty's Landing were easy enough to find, but trying to find the rock at the sandy shore behind Mr. Dean's house where the bass struck at my mother's cigarette butt was more of a challenge. The sandy little beach was now an invisible part of the woods that were growing ever closer to the edge of the river. We finally found the rock but it seemed as if it was much farther away from the river than it should have been.

We took a walk away from the river where the path from our house to the river should have been, but I had the eerie feeling that we were now intruders and hoped no one would see us and tell us to get off their property. The tall pine tree where our "tree house" used to be was gone as were the many other tall pines that followed Dean's property line to the river. Only one or two of them still remained. It was then that the true realization that all I have written of in this book took place more than fifty years before! It was a small wonder that anything from our past remained at all.

We *were* intruders! The world that we had grown up in did not exist anymore. Nature and man had stolen it away and it would never exist again except in our minds and in these written words. It had been wiped away so completely that it was difficult for us to find tiny remnants to prove to ourselves that it had existed in reality and not in our minds. The landscape was not the only thing that had changed. Only a few of the people we had known still lived nearby or, indeed, were still living at all.

Not only is The Cove gone, but so are the stately elm trees by the bridge over Johnson Brook; victims of the infamous Dutch elm disease. Baltimore Orioles used to build their basket-like nests high up near their tops. What man hadn't taken away, nature did.

Upstream and across the river; sitting proudly atop our favorite shopping center, the Veazie town dump, is the Veazie Salmon Club. There is a beautiful view from up there of our former fishing waters below the dam. I suspect that many of its members may not have an inkling of what lies buried deep beneath its floors. I hope the rats have all departed.

Downstream from there on the opposite shore of the Penobscot and occupying Maude Folsom's former home-site (the lady I used to borrow the rowboat from) is the Eddington version of the Veazie Salmon Club. I feel sorry for both clubs. I wonder if any of their members will ever be able to catch an Atlantic Salmon in the Penobscot River again, then take it home and enjoy a salmon dinner.

The Cove and the Penobscot River held a special meaning to me that was akin to the relationship of a father or a very close friend. It had always been there for me as a safe haven when I sorely needed it as a young man. It was as if after I ceased to need it, it had died. The last day I was there, I felt as if I was attending the funeral of an old friend and I was the only one who mourned.

THE END

Bud Simpson (Former Mainuh!) Logan, Ohio, 2006

The Handsome Brute to the right is me at around age two. To my right is my sister Joan with her arm around another sister, Dolores. It was probably taken by my mother, Stella Simpson. We were in front of my Grandfather Roy Mann's house on North Main Street in North Brewer. His house was just a few houses up North Main Street from ours and on the opposite side of the road. The road is in the background to the left.

P.S.—I've had a haircut since then.

This is my brother, Trevor, with a wild friend, a young snapping turtle. This picture was also taken by my mother. He is standing in our front yard on North Main street. He probably brought this young turtle home from the Penobscot River behind the house or possibly from Johnson Brook about a quarter of a mile behind him. As you can tell, he wasn't as good looking as me.

This is me. It was taken by my mother the same day as the
preceding picture of my brother, Trevor. I didn't have a turtle,
but I think Trevor let me hold his, so that may be why my arms
are missing. As you can see, I wasn't lying about our looks.

This thin, wide-eyed fella is me at about the age of eighteen. I had just stepped into the kitchen from our front room. I think my cousin "Sib" Orcutt snapped this photo with my camera. I have slightly less hair today. I don't look quite as innocent, either.

This is my long-suffering mother, Estelle Marguerite (Mann) Simpson. I got her to pose on the back "porch" for this shot with my red felt hunting hat on her head and my Winchester Model 94, .32 Special in her hand. Trevor shot the fox, but we can't remember who got the deer. The photo was made with my very first 35mm camera; a cheap Kodak Pony. It didn't seem so cheap at the time. Those are her clothes lines visible behind the porch

This is the first Simpson home on North Main Street in Brewer. It was built on a rock foundation and had no running water. I don't see any electric lines coming to it, so it may not have had electricity at the time this photo was taken. The tear in the photo's upper left hides a lean-to style addition that became a kitchen. My father's Model-A Ford is in the driveway. Some of the trees in the picture are still growing there today.

This picture was taken in the Forties. The house has had "improvements" that allowed for more bedrooms upstairs. Unfortunately, this was as finished as the house ever got. The tarred paper and cedar lath siding didn't provide much insulation during Maine's long and cold winters.

The above view is of the Eddington Bend area of the Penobscot River in 1949. Why it is called "The Bend" is obvious from this photo. The Cove and Johnson Brook are visible near the bottom of the picture and the Veazie Dam is shown at the top.

(From an aerial view of the Cove and river provided by the James W. Sewell Company, Old Town, Maine 04468)

This is a closer view of the Cove area. North Main Street runs by from left to right. My home was located to the extreme right in this photo where North Main runs out of the picture. It blends in well with the scenery.

(From a James W. Sewell Company photo.)

A late springtime view of the Veazie Dam in the early fifties. This was taken from the Eddington side with the Town of Veazie in the background.

This close-up view of the dam was taken from atop the fishway on the Eddington side of the Penobscot River.

Looking towards Bangor from the Brewer side of the Bangor Hydro Electric dam. The tide is in and the world famous Bangor salmon pool is slightly downstream from here.

Another view of the Bangor dam taken in the late forties. The tide is out in this view allowing me to walk out into the river on the exposed rocks.

This is the Bangor Salmon Pool. It was actually located on the Brewer side of the river. More than a dozen anglers are trying their luck from shore. This was back when you could actually take an Atlantic Salmon home with you and have it for dinner.

A view of the Penobscot River from behind my house in North Brewer taken in the early spring in the fifties. The ice is just beginning to break up.

Another view From farther down stream and above the sandy beach behind Mr. Dean's house. This was taken a few weeks later after the ice has left this part of the river.

Another fifties view of the river from near the sandy beach behind Mr. Dean's house. It was taken on the same day as the previous photo.

Looking upstream from Johnson Brook in the early fifties. This is directly across the street from my house. It is springtime and the water level is perfect for the annual sucker run. The brook has made a sharp turn from the south (to the right) at this point. Note the American Elm tree top center. Dutch Elm Disease killed it in later years.

Looking upstream on Johnson Brook where it turns sharply from the previous photo. This photo was taken on the same day. I am standing on the top edge of a small gravel pit.

A view of Picked Diamond in the early fifties. This shows the normal height of water in the river at that time. After the Bangor dam was breached and later torn out, the waters never reached this height again except possibly during early spring freshets.

This is Picked Diamond as it is today. The view is from across the mouth of the Cove at the base of the pine grove. As you can see, the Penobscot's waters are at least fifteen feet below the base of the rock. It's hard to believe that kids of days past swung out on ropes tied to the trees behind the rock and dropped into the river's waters for a swim.

This is an aerial view of the Cove from a few years back. It still looks like this today with even more trees and bushes growing up through it. I have drawn in the old borders where its waters were backed up before the hurricanes and breaches in the Bangor dam destroyed it.

(From a USGS Photo)

An aerial view showing where the old Simpson home was located on North Main Street. The original house was torn down in the mid fifties and was replaced by the one in the lower right of this photo. Mr. Dean lived in the house in the center of the photo.

This view of the remains of the Cove was taken by me in October of 2006. Picked Diamond can be seen at the tree line to the right. The light colored foliage shows where the waters of the Cove used to be. The dark foliage to the left is the pine grove.

North Main Street and the Penobscot River snake by the Cove area . The remains of the Cove are located beneath the light colored trees near the center of the photo. Across the Penobscot River is the Bangor Hydro power house.

This aerial view Shows Johnson Brook across the road from where I lived. It flows under North Main Street bridge in the upper right and then beneath it and into the Cove. The sharp left turn at the bottom of the picture is where the gravel pit was located.

(From a USGS Photo)

The remains of the Bangor Hydro-electric dam in Bangor, Maine. It was taken in 2006. Its destruction was not only the final nail in the coffin for the Cove but also for the world famous Bangor Salmon Pool as it used to be.

Salmon fishermen congregate on both sides of the river in Veazie and Eddington now and not in Bangor as much. This fisherman enjoys an afternoon of fishing from the Eddington club house. The Veazie dam is in the background. This is now the head of tide once again as it was before European explorers and modern man appeared on the scene.

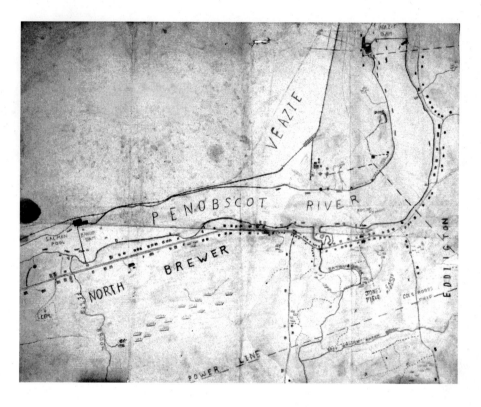

This is a map of area in this book. My brother, Trevor, drew it in the fifties. Although it is difficult to read because of its age, the X's show where he shot deer and the fish icons show where he found the best fishing to be for him.

All photos taken by the author or his Mother, Stella Simpson, unless otherwise noted.